Every
Home a
Foundation

Every Home a Foundation

EXPERIENCING GOD THROUGH YOUR EVERYDAY ROUTINES

PHYLICIA MASONHEIMER

W PUBLISHING GROUP

AN IMPRINT OF THOMAS NELSON

Every Home a Foundation

© 2024 Phylicia Masonheimer

Published in Nashville, Tennessee, by W Publishing, an imprint of Thomas Nelson.

Thomas Nelson titles may be purchased in bulk for educational, business, fundraising, or sales promotional use. For information, please email SpecialMarkets@ThomasNelson.com.

Unless otherwise noted, Scripture quotations are taken from the ESV® Bible (The Holy Bible, English Standard Version®). Copyright © 2001 by Crossway, a publishing ministry of Good News Publishers. Used by permission. All rights reserved.

Scripture quotations marked NASB are taken from the New American Standard Bible® (NASB). Copyright © 1960, 1962, 1963, 1968, 1971, 1972, 1973, 1975, 1977, 1995, 2020 by The Lockman Foundation. Used by permission. www.Lockman.org

Scripture quotations marked NIV are taken from the Holy Bible, New International Version®, NIV®. Copyright © 1973, 1978, 1984, 2011 by Biblica, Inc.® Used by permission of Zondervan. All rights reserved worldwide. www.zondervan.com. The "NIV" and "New International Version" are trademarks registered in the United States Patent and Trademark Office by Biblica, Inc.®

Scripture quotations marked NLT are taken from the Holy Bible, New Living Translation. Copyright © 1996, 2004, 2015 by Tyndale House Foundation. Used by permission of Tyndale House Ministries, Carol Stream, Illinois 60188. All rights reserved.

ISBN 978-0-7852-9229-6 (audiobook)
ISBN 978-0-7852-9228-9 (ePub)
ISBN 978-0-7852-9226-5 (HC)

Library of Congress Control Number: 2024944745

Printed in the United States of America
24 25 26 27 28 LBC 5 4 3 2 1

This book is dedicated to all the homes and hearts that shaped me, and to all the doors, tables, and affections opened to our family over the years.

I never thought I'd be raising kids
with the kids I grew up with.
These narrow streets closed me in
and I escaped them: "I won't settle"
turned into "I won't settle down,"
and then I did.
Right back where I started.
TikTok calls it failure,
shows me waterfalls in Bali,
bikini bodies and brunches,
far from my little city and little babies
living my boomerang life.

But what TikTok doesn't show
of the town I grew up in
are narrow streets of people who know me
whose love has closed me in.
An embrace instead of escape,
a place to settle and settle down.
The limits I once tried to break
are my safety,
right back where I started.
Now my babies toddle on tiny legs
beside babies with last names
as familiar as my own.

They mocked us for coming back,
called it settling. I guess it is.
Settling for front porch visits,
the barista's smile (she's my cousin),

the winding roads of youthful risk,
a hollered "hello!" across the park,
knowing the postmaster's name.
To make a home, you have to settle.
And I settled for raising kids
with the kids I grew up with
in the town we grew up in.
Not backwards; full circle.
Like arms in an embrace.

"HOME," PHYLICIA D. MASONHEIMER

Contents

Contents

Introduction

Confessions of an Unlikely Homebody

ONE WOULD THINK I ALWAYS LOVED BEING HOME.

I work from home. My husband works from home.

We have a small farm—a *home*stead.

We *home*school our children.

"Home" is my favorite place to be, but I didn't come to my current view of it by being a homebody. The opposite, actually.

Early in my adulthood, I was a college adviser, recruiting students for my alma mater, traveling around the United States to conferences and other glamorous things. And when I resigned, I continued to travel for my growing ministry (I am the founder of Every Woman a Theologian, an interdenominational ministry teaching theology and apologetics to lay Christians): Texas, California, Virginia, Missouri, Arkansas, Ohio, Massachusetts. I loved the thrill of meeting readers, opening God's Word, and worshiping alongside women of faith. And I still do. But a few years ago, God called me to end my ten-year stint of work travel and focus my attention at home.

Over that decade, I got married, moved three times, and had three babies. Life changed a lot. When I stopped traveling for work, it dawned on me that despite all my home systems, routines, and homeschooling, it was possible to be home *a lot* . . . yet not home at all. My mind was not content there. Each month had one or two speaking engagements or commitments to pull me out of the house—away from my young children, away from the repetitive work of dishes and laundry for the *real, important* work of ministry. I lived in the home, I even loved my home, but ultimately my attitude toward home was one of ingratitude.

Hi, I'm Phylicia. And I'm a woman hemmed in by home in all the best ways.

Before you think I quit ministry, put on a dress, and took up sourdough-bread making: think again! I still work almost forty hours a week leading a team of ten amazing employees—including my wonderful husband, Josh. I still write books and teach (in my living room instead of on a stage). I didn't leave my calling to love home well. I just learned to view it differently. I had to take back the purpose I'd lost—a purpose that does not require a full travel schedule, an outside job, a fancy kitchen, or a big bank account to achieve. I needed a refresh on my *theology* of home.

Home was important to me theoretically; I liked the idea of home, the picture I had in my head of calming routines and strong community, but once I was actually within those four walls my mind lived elsewhere. This wasn't helped by the pressure of social media, which told me to be anywhere *but* home. Travel seemed glamorous (even though it exhausted me). Taking the kids on another outing seemed necessary (even though they thrived on consistent routines). Having a packed schedule away from my living room seemed like the grown-up choice (even though I came home tired). Home was for boring people, and I didn't want to be boring, so I didn't stay home.

My vanity—a desire to be applauded for how busy I was and how exciting my life appeared—drove me out of my house. My theology of home was shaped more by pop culture and unhealthy work ethics than by the Word of God. Sure, I took care of the laundry and dishes, planned meals, and entertained. But when I look back at my attitude toward home in those early days, I see a person desperate to make herself exciting but ending up unfulfilled. The truth I didn't know then, and know now, is this: a biblical theology of home brings out the deep, abiding joy of a "boring" life. I have long believed the home is a vital place for Christian believers. It is the primary seat of discipleship, where people are most comfortable, safe, and freely themselves. But we are all forgetful sometimes. My years of saying yes without question led to months and weeks of time away from home, not because I always felt called to what I was doing but because I unconsciously believed what I was doing was more meaningful than the unseen work of the kitchen and living rooms. This book lays out a theology of home that is not the rigidly gender-roled model of the "tradwife" movement, nor the anti-domestic diatribe of secular feminism. It is not a book about motherhood (though I am a mother to three); it is not a book about professional work (though I am the CEO of a business and ministry).

This is a book about seeing home as a place of purpose.

This is a book about living with purpose in the home.

Forming a theology of home doesn't require homeschooling, working from home, wearing certain clothes, or baking bread without yeast. Theology is the study of God: His nature and how He interacts with us. A theology of home teaches us God's *desire for* and *purpose within* the places we live. If you're reading this, you probably have a home: a shared apartment, an old duplex, a parent's renovated basement, or a cul-de-sac craftsman. All homes require labor, usually the kind we like to put off because it's not exciting— but it's work that matters immensely to God.

I wonder if some of us fear mundanity. We resent our homes because they represent all the "not yets" of our lives. We wake up each day seeing things that need fixing and redoing, or we're reminded of the lifestyle we're told we should afford. Home makes us feel like failures, so we close our eyes to it and don't invest much effort. I don't know about you, but I don't want to waste years of my life resenting the place I live, the place where most of my memories are stored. I want to do the work of home with joy, and I want to remember it just that way—*as a joy*. Not that I will ever choose matching socks over going out on the town, but that when matching socks comes around, I know there's an eternal purpose in the mundane tasks of my daily life.

Dishes, laundry, raking, cleaning: culture tells us they don't matter, but life can't run without them. Like it or not, daily tasks are part of living, *evidence* of living. I would rather see God in them, a glimpse of eternity in everything I put my hand to, than miss out on what He might be saying because I thought this work was below my attention.

As you read through this book, you'll encounter stories from my own life, peeks into the homes of friends and family, jaunts through history and literature, practical tips for creating routines and rhythms, poems and liturgies. Our homes reflect our values in diverse ways, and this book reflects the theology of home via several different media. All the poems and liturgies included in this book are written by me, unless otherwise noted.

Whether you're single and a college student, newly married and climbing the corporate ladder, an empty nester with a big house that feels far too silent, a mama to a fresh little babe: I hope this book leads you to appreciate the work of your hands at home because God certainly does.

PART I

A Theology of Home

CHAPTER 1

A Peaceful Habitation

In a tender place the dawn glows blue
dousing snow in cobalt swathes
until wings beat sun above the woods
and all that lived in dark is lost.

The music of this breaking morning
is scraping stools and stumbling feet;
the croak, reluctant coffeepot;
the sizzle, iron over heat.

We make the day while sun is shining
our work below, it journeys lonely
observing on its steady path
what we call normal—God calls holy.
"NORMAL," *PDM*

GRANDMA'S HOUSE WAS AN HOUR AND A HALF AWAY, A winding drive past shivering hardwoods and old Michigan farms. We'd turn right at the river and see the house she grew up in, white with black shutters, its surprised eyes looking past Wooden Shoe Lake. We'd pull into Grandma's driveway and pile into her house—a place filled with the scent of Maxwell House coffee, roast beef, and apple pie. We'd lie on the floor vents to feel the heat and skate down the linoleum floor while Grandma piled our plates with more food: "You're hardly eating anything! Eat up so you don't blow away!"

Grandma's house was *comfort*. It was warm, squishy, filling, sweet, and safe.

But what if I told you that Grandma's house was a single-wide trailer with paneled walls, cheap vinyl floors, an ancient yellow bathtub, and a galley kitchen?

That's right. The trailer was a formative part of my childhood and eventual view of the home. No fancy tile kitchen or quaint cottage facade. No stretching acreage or attached garage. Just a place to feel safe and loved, to be fed and attended to—to chase toads, dig holes, and make cookies. The smell of Maxwell House still takes me back.

My grandma was divorced, never remarried, and made her money running garage sales and cleaning houses. Her existence was as humble as her home. Though she no longer lives there, I drive by her trailer from time to time. It looks so much smaller than it did when I was ten, running up the porch stairs, swinging wide the door as she yelled, "Ohhhh, hello!" Whether hunting for toads in the backyard, sifting through the bin of garage-sale toys in the spare bedroom, or sneakily watching *Power Rangers* on the bedroom TV, Grandma's house was familiar and safe, not because of what it looked like but because of the person who lived there. Grandma loved us. Her trailer might have been small, but it was impeccably clean, and there was always food on the table and a loud welcome at the door. Grandma loved us in the way she knew best: by cooking, cleaning, mending, giving.

> A home holds up the people within it.

If you were to close your eyes and imagine, I am confident you could think of a place—a home—where you felt like I did: safe, loved, attended to. Maybe it was the home your parents built; maybe it was the home of a friend. That home was more than a house to you—it was a place of refuge. More than the four walls holding it up, a home holds up the people within it, covering them with grace and peace.

Homes and *houses* are not the same. You can have a beautiful mansion empty of true purpose and affection. You can have a tiny trailer full of love and safety. "Better a dry crust with peace and quiet than a house full of feasting, with strife" (Proverbs 17:1 NIV). A home can be built with the sparest materials as long as the heart behind it is unified with God's mission.

In her trailer my grandma loved us through a humble home

and mundane tasks—primarily cooking and cleaning. If Grandma showed up, you knew there would be an entire three-course meal and a perfectly cleaned kitchen by noontime! She attributed a greater value, a meaning or blessing, to humble things. And she taught—mostly by accident—that an eternal purpose is woven into the fabric of home and all its tasks.

Looking back, my grandma's home and her actions there weren't the only ones that impacted me. There were others:

- The small cottage of my friend's parents, where the house always smelled like baked goods, and we sat in inflatable chairs and giggled over American Girl books for hours.
- The sprawling house of my college Bible study leader, an empty nester with a lovely kitchen she used to bless the women she led.
- The second-floor apartment of my single friend who invited me for coffee when I was a young mom with babies in tow.
- The historic home of our small-group host couple, who opened their door to eight adults and fourteen children every week—while their home was under massive renovation.
- The home I grew up in, built with my father's own hands and filled with beauty and goodness by my mother.

None of these homes were perfect. Some were small. Some were under construction. All of the families had pain, loss, and brokenness somewhere in their history. But the people in these homes had something in common: they saw home, and the mundane tasks within it, as something worthy of their best. They gave their best at home and invited others (me!) to participate in the blessing of their faithfulness. They saw the daily routines of making food, cleaning up, and opening their door as a way to love. And I was loved because of them. I mourn to think of the loss experienced if these people had waited for a bigger home or less to do before inviting me in.

Though I grew up in a home full of love, my parents worked hard to provide it for us. They allowed Christ to redeem their histories and tried to build something completely new. Chances are you, too, have been affected by the brokenness of home in a sinful world. Even the word *home* may be a trigger for you—not a word of comfort and peace but a reminder of anxiety, fear, and isolation. Maybe you didn't grow up in a home that felt safe. In fact, home was the opposite of safe. You spent as much time away from it as you could. Maybe you grew up in a home that was distant, cold, and lonely. No one was invited in; sometimes you felt like you didn't even belong. Maybe you had a parent who did not care well for the home, so you had no example and now feel like you're drowning. There is room for all our stories here, because God does not leave us homeless in heart, wandering without communion, unseen in our pain. God is in the business of redemption, and the homes He builds cannot be undermined.

Home matters to God. It is the center of true discipleship.

THE HISTORY OF HOME

The very first home was a garden. In Genesis 1–2 God builds a home for His people. It has food, provision, work to be done, rest to be had, and most of all, community! God Himself walked with Adam and Eve in the cool of the day (Genesis 3:8). God's desire was to dwell in perfect unity with His people so they could experience a free and fulfilling relationship with Him and the world He created. But as we discover in Genesis 3, sin invaded the first home. The unity, safety, and love God intended for home were all shattered in a moment. God could not dwell with His people in their rebellious state, the labor of earth was exhausting and resistant, and the labor of life-giving—fertility, childbirth, and parenthood—was now full of pain. The perfect home was broken.

The fall of humanity broke what God created, but God wasn't done. In Genesis 3, He promised to send the seed of the woman to crush the Enemy for good. He promised a Messiah, a Savior, to reconcile all things to Himself and redeem the painful choice of mankind. In the meantime, God did not leave; He revealed Himself in Old Testament history, dwelling among His people in a tabernacle and a temple until Jesus Christ, the Messiah, arrived. God's mission is to build a home for His people. He began the story with a home in a garden and He ends it with a home in a heavenly city. Hebrews 13:14 tells us, "For here we do not have an enduring city, but we are looking for the city that is to come" (NIV). God's heart is for His people to find the kind of belonging a home should provide—and to create that belonging for others. Home matters immensely to God.

> The LORD's curse is on the house of the wicked,
>   but he blesses the dwelling of the righteous.
> (Proverbs 3:33)

The revelation of God's character through Scripture was first passed down orally. It was communicated to families in their homes—not in church buildings—as they lived, worked, and worshiped together. After the exodus from Egypt, the Jewish people were gathered at Mount Sinai to receive God's law: a law outlining how to live well in communion with God and in community with other people. During the wandering years, Israel's "home" was in tents and God's story was passed down through the generations in anticipation of the homes they would one day possess in the promised land. Home throughout these decades (and before) was the center of discipleship.

When Israel settled in Canaan and built homes, they were

commanded to choose whether they would make God the center of their homes or not. They were entering a wild and untamed land filled with people who hated God. To live well in such a land, Israel had to be clear about their purpose, starting at home. Joshua spoke to this in his challenge to the people: "If it is evil in your eyes to serve the LORD, choose this day whom you will serve, whether the gods your fathers served in the region beyond the River, or the gods of the Amorites in whose land you dwell. But as for me and my house, we will serve the LORD" (24:15).

Joshua, the Israelite leader after Moses, set an example of leadership in his home. His household (his family, servants, and everyone who lived under his roof) was touched by his commitment to God, which set the tone for the entire home.

In the nomadic world of ancient Israel, home and work life were not separate. They were united in every possible way (and in some cultures this unity continues today). When Joshua stated that his household would serve the Lord, he meant everyone who lived under his roof would do so in *all of their ways*. Deuteronomy further supports this when Moses spoke to parents about their discipleship responsibility in the home: "These commandments that I give you today are to be on your hearts. Impress them on your children. Talk about them when you sit at home and when you walk along the road, when you lie down and when you get up. Tie them as symbols on your hands and bind them on your foreheads. Write them on the doorframes of your houses and on your gates" (6:6–9 NIV).

Ancient Israelites lived with the home at the center of life and godliness. During the wandering years, the camps of each tribe encircled the tabernacle, God's dwelling place. Each tribe of Israel, and each family tent within the tribe, lived life with God at the center. This was further reflected by the Levitical law. Personal actions affected every other person in the home community and, on a larger scale, their neighbors and friends. Those "abstract" laws in Leviticus were intended to create a community based on love, honor, justice, and welcome—beginning first at home in interpersonal relationships and extending outward to the foreigner and alien (25:35). Joshua's allegiance to the Lord was a prototype of how every Israelite house was to function: healthy relationships with others stemming from an intimate relationship with God, beginning with those under your own roof (or your tent).

If we read further into the Old Testament, we see that Joshua's devotion to God at home was not imitated by Israel at large. Instead of choosing the righteousness God offered through His law, Israel chose the brokenness of sin. They adopted the identity of the nations around them, along with their sinful practices, instead of the goodness and unity of life with God. And God, who had chosen Israel as His "home" (a light to the nations), gave them the consequences of their own evil choices. Israel lost the promised land, their home with God, to live in exile among the Assyrians and Babylonians. But even in this place, even after grievous sin, God called Israel to make themselves a home:

> Thus says the LORD of hosts, the God of Israel, to all the exiles whom I have sent into exile from Jerusalem to Babylon: Build houses and live in them; plant gardens and eat their produce. Take wives and have sons and daughters; take wives for your sons, and give your daughters in marriage, that they may bear sons and daughters; multiply there, and do not decrease. But seek the welfare of the city where I have sent you into exile, and pray to the LORD on its behalf, for in its welfare you will find your welfare. (Jeremiah 29:4–7)

According to God, *home* is possible even in broken places. *Home* is possible even when we've sinned, or when our parents paved a path we never would have chosen. God is in the business of home-building, and when He is the foundation, we will always build well.

Coming out of the medieval era, European homelife was surprisingly similar to ancient Israel's. People worked near or in their living space. Agriculture was the central, if not primary, industry, and if you worked the land, you probably lived on or near it. In homes, bedrooms were not a reality for any but the extremely wealthy (and even the rich did not always adopt them). Families slept together in a main "hall" and, in the lower classes, worked together to survive. If you were self-employed or a skilled laborer, your place of business was often attached to your home in some way (think: *Johnny Tremain*'s silver shop, *Great Expectations*'s blacksmithing forge, and in the twentieth century, Corrie ten Boom's apartment above her father's watchmaking storefront). From mothers to daughters to fathers to sons, everyone in the lower and middle class worked to survive: laundry, cooking, gardening, tending animals, sewing, mending, knitting, woodworking—the things we think of as hobbies today were essential to simply live.

Everyone labored together in the home. This continued through the eighteenth century both in Europe and in the newly settled New World. Settlers like the Separatist Pilgrims lived in communities where home, work, and faith were integrated and inseparable. Puritan settlements in New England emphasized the impact of faith on both work life and homelife. Living well at home was an act of stewardship, and the ethic one brought to their professional sphere carried over to things like laundry, cooking, cleaning, and caring for animals. "Do all things as unto the Lord," in the Puritan mind, was more than a concept; it was a lifestyle.

Everything changed for the American home during the Industrial Revolution. Machines made man-made items more inefficient and, eventually, obsolete. With inventions like the steam engine, cotton gin, and electricity, "better, faster, stronger" took priority. As factories took over the work landscape, a divide began to form between work and home. People left their farms and personal businesses to work in cities; they left the home to head to the factory, bank, or railroad. The work of the home, once done in an almost-egalitarian fashion by both men and women, was now mostly relegated to wives and daughters. With husbands and sons working long hours to provide, the bulk of home tasks fell to female members of the family. With the Industrial Revolution, it was possible to make more money than ever before. Perhaps because of the value placed on financial success, the work of the home—non-income producing—came to be seen as less valuable.

As World War I and World War II crashed onto the national scene, more women left homes to work in factories. Poor women had always worked, but with the war effort there was a new note of admiration for working women—they were helping win the war! Perhaps this moved more women of wealthier classes to the workforce. American culture realized women were not just stand-ins for men; women were effective, efficient, and intelligent workers. When WWII ended and women returned to the home (now in the 1950s), a rising discontent began to pervade the women of America. Their experience working in a place where their contribution was measurable, observable, and impactful, coupled with the invention of time-saving home-management machines like the microwave, refrigerator, dishwasher, and vacuum, made home tasks both less time-consuming and less appealing. By the time of the sexual revolution in the 1960s, no one needed to tell American women that tending the home was boring, obsolete, and fake. They felt it. The *Leave It to Beaver* ideal proved hollow, and feminism promised something more: *women could have it all.* They could join the workforce, work as well as men, and enjoy all the rights that men did. The work of the home came to be seen as oppressive and limiting.

Before the sexual revolution, habits of the home (how to clean, plan, make meals, grow your own food, mend what was broken) were handed down generation to generation. We were taught how to peel potatoes in the same way we were taught to walk. My own grandmother taught me how to scrub a baseboard, clean as I cooked, and fold fitted sheets. Her mother, a rural Michigan farmwife and mother of eight, taught *her*. And Great-Grandma Pearl's mother was off the boat from the Netherlands, never spoke a "lick of English" (as my grandma put it), but probably knew how to scrub tile and get all the food out of the oven at the same time. My point is: before the sexual revolution, the shattering impact of the world wars, and the Industrial Revolution, the family handed down an *appreciation* for the home. Though by no means idyllic or even moral, without even thinking about it, parents and grand-parents (who not uncommonly lived all together) handed down the knowledge of home and its purpose. Most of the time they did this out of sheer necessity; they wanted to survive. But even in neces-sity, this handing down of home legacy built a sense of purpose and identity in the home.

There are many other factors I don't have time to address: latchkey kids left at home while both parents worked; the scatter-ing of family units as children moved far away from their city of origin; the evolution of essential life skills to hobbies; the prom-ise that women really *could* have it all: a successful career, an awesome marriage, a family, community, and home; the differ-ences ethnicity and culture play in family dynamics (for example, metropolitan white Americans are less likely to live near or with family than Black, Hispanic, or rurally located white Americans are[1]). Through a combination of many factors, the Western home became a place to crash, a place to recover from the world—not a place to serve or prepare for it. Home lost its purpose, and the work of the home lost its meaning. The generations who believed domestic arts to be oppressive did not hand them down to their daughters and sons (a *Good Housekeeping* survey in 2018 found that millennials only know how to do eleven out of eighteen once-essential household skills[2]). When those daughters decided they wanted *more* than the workaholism of the generation before, they were left overwhelmed and empty-handed, trying to learn home skills they were never taught while *still* working a full-time job.

This brings us to today. Extended families are scattered across long distances, leaving young parents with little support. Home is something to show off on Instagram or HGTV, not something to share with people across a table. Our schedules are so jam-packed, our perfectionism so suffocating, we can't open our doors to the family across the street. Domestic tasks are seen as unnecessary and yet when we abandon them, we feel claustrophobic, overwhelmed, cluttered, and sad.

This isn't to say that life was better, or perfect, in the 1700s. I enjoy my conveniences as much as the next person! Even when Western culture had a stronger centralized family and an appreciation for homelife and industry, many homes were just as broken as they are today. Without a Christian theology of home, the most purposeful homelife can become abusive. The most intimate homelife can become codependent and controlling. Observing history shows us how we got here, but it doesn't mean that homelife in the eighteenth, nineteenth, or twentieth centuries in America was innately better. There were different challenges in a different time. What we *can* do is identify what has changed across the last four centuries and ask ourselves: *Has our view of home really progressed as a society and church, or have we gone too far?* We don't have to return to the nineteenth century, but we should critique and question a view of home that sees "real life" as everything outside the door.

HOME AS THE CENTER OF DISCIPLESHIP

The home has changed a lot since Israel's day and not just because of air-conditioning! How did we get from that original vision—home as a place of intimacy, purpose, and industry—to seeing home as boring, overwhelming, and suited only to loungewear? At times in history, home was considered more central to society; people worked to survive and the home-work divide was not as wide as it is today. While home in history is by no means perfect, we can turn to the past to understand the changes to our perception of it.

A quick scroll through social media for the search term "home" tells me that it is both a place that overwhelms us ("The key to a clean house is to clean it twenty-four hours a day") and also a place we never want to leave ("I love canceled plans!"). We long for community ("The real miracle is that Jesus had twelve close friends in His thirties") but we don't invite others in ("My house is a mess"). Let's talk more about these feelings.

Home as a place of overwhelm: Unlike a desk at work, which we tidy upon leaving and find the same upon return, our homes devolve into chaos just by being used. My mom called it the "lived-in look." Homes require maintenance to counteract the mess of daily use. All of us have to organize, scrub, and pick up the living room. Unfortunately, many people are not taught *how* to care for their living space. As the days unfold, tasks pile one on top the other until the chore list is so long, we don't even know where to start.

Home as a place of isolation: As a social introvert, I like canceled plans as much as the next person. But I also know the importance of community and friendship. Some days I make myself leave the house because I know it's the best thing for me; other times I head to a coffee date or a meetup because it's the best thing for the other person. Homes are not hermitages. To thrive as a place of discipleship and growth, our homes must be centered on more than just our own pleasures and comforts. We have to leave our homes to form relationships that will fill our homes with goodness.

Home as a place of community: I've already said home is the seat of discipleship, and discipleship is an active form of community. I like to think of discipleship as intentional, focused spiritual friendship. I'm a member of the millennial generation, and millennials love to *talk* about community, but living it out is a lot harder to do. Godly community is not just "hangout time." It is deeper, broader, and more gracious than that. Godly community (discipleship in action) faces down the hard questions, invites a broad range of people, and gives grace for imperfection and failure. The home is where such depth, breadth, and growth are facilitated.

Home as a place of welcome: We've been sold a lie that true connection can only happen in perfect houses. We've been sold another lie: homes are only for *our* pleasure and comfort—no one else's. These two lies together keep us from opening our doors. We will have an entire chapter about this later on.

There is an unrecognized inner conflict regarding the home that is pulling at men and women, Christian and non-Christian alike. We want to enjoy the places we live, but we feel ill-equipped to care for them. We want a thriving, deep community, but we want other people to do the inviting. We think of home as a safe place, a refuge, but see its tasks as boring and mundane. We still have to fold laundry, make meals, clean floors, and wash dishes. Christians are spiritually *divided* from their homes. The things done in church, Bible study, or on a stage are seen as ministry and spiritually valuable; the things done in the home (whether cleaning tasks, discipleship of children, or hospitality) are seen as extra physical tasks that have no real spiritual impact. This could not be further from the truth.

We've been trained not to see the value of home; we've been taught that home is a burden and its care an impediment to real life. But God said all work matters (1 Corinthians 10:31), and our homes, the place where we should be free and vulnerable, matter immensely to Him.

A biblical theology of home is the answer to all home problems across all centuries. It frees us to not just *enjoy* the place we live but to live with purpose and dignity. What if we can recapture what was lost to the rugged individualism of the American dream? What if we could worship God through dishes, laundry, mopping, cooking, mending, and hospitality; and what if there was truly a way to show up to our homes from a place of peace?

I say "what if," but I can make you a promise: there is a way. *And it's God's way home.* It's grace-based, rest-filled, adaptable, and free. And it's more than just physical—it's a spiritual practice! The Christian home is an image of both a *coming* spiritual reality and the *existing* spiritual reality of our family, the church. We are part of something bigger than ourselves. Our homes should reflect the priorities of Christ, our foundation and cornerstone of the church.

John Tweeddale says this: "The home is not a neutral zone for acting upon baseless desires, nor is it simply a bastion for maintaining traditional values. One of the primary purposes of the home is to cultivate Christlike virtues that animate who we are in private and facilitate what we do in public."[3]

The home is where it all begins, where it all dwells, and where it all ends. Through Christ we can heal a home experience that was hurtful, chaotic, or unsafe. Through Christ we can build a home for ourselves and others that is everything our childhood home was not. Through Christ we have a cornerstone for every beautiful thing we build. And on such a rock, that house will stand.

> The home is where it all begins, where it all dwells, and where it all ends.

Grandma's trailer wasn't much to look at, but it was much to my ten-year-old heart. Her table was brown and bland and, to be honest, sometimes her mashed potatoes were too (she didn't believe in salt). But she handed me a set of skills I still use today. Grandma handed me her heart, though it looked a lot like a mop and a roasting pan. What if love looks like that? Can we see the home and all it entails as not just a place to be loved but as a *way* to love? I think we can.

> My people will abide in a peaceful habitation, in
> secure dwellings,
> and in quiet resting places. (Isaiah 32:18)

CHAPTER 2

Loving the Home You Have

Everything I have was first in
a treasury inaccessible to me.
Unlocked by grace,
bestowed by kindness,
given with mercy
to be re-gifted again and again—
pressed down and running over
like oil too voluminous to be
contained.
Rather than fear the gifts
and resist the goodness,
I accept them both with open hands,
then leave them open.
And through the sun on our hills
and the softness of a smile,
the joy in a glass and fruit of our hands,
they also can taste and see:
He is good. He is good indeed.

"HOSPITALITY," PDM

EVERY YEAR DURING EASTER I CALL GOOD FRIDAY "Black Friday." I confused them once and my mind can't undo it. For some reason "Black Friday" sounds more appropriate for a crucifixion than for a day dedicated to mass materialism. I've always found it highly ironic that Black Friday, a day dedicated to shopping, comes less than twenty-four hours after we gather to give thanks for what we have. And while I have been known to participate in a few good sales over the years, I generally try to avoid the whiplash of thanking God one day and spending hundreds of dollars the next; I just can't make that shift so quickly!

That said, it's tempting to scroll through the endless gift guides: for him, for her, for the kids. I love seeing the recommendations. I tell myself I do in fact need that ice machine; the one in our fridge keeps clogging up. Or maybe an air fryer instead? Those are all the rage. *Could I use some cute pajamas? I'm sure Josh is tired of me wandering about the house looking like the ghost of grandmas past in my floor-length white nightgown.* And there are the books, for which I have no limits on budget or amount.

In the midst of these gift guide suggestions, there's always one slide that stops me: *for the home.* Here I find sheets, candles, acrylic chairs, centerpieces, cast iron pans, wooden spoons, trendy trash cans, and throw pillows all beckoning my attention. All promising me: *Once you buy this, your home will be worthy.*

We like to blame the internet and social media for our discontent; after all, these picture-perfect houses are always in front of us. But what if social media isn't the problem? What if it simply reveals a problem that was already there?

The shiny images of beautiful homes we see online tweak something in our hearts. It's not that beautiful homes are wrong (they aren't), espresso machines are sinful (not true), or a perfectly laid table is unrealistic (for some people, it's not). These items are amoral; they do not possess a morality in and of themselves. The issue lies in how they interact with our *souls.* The twinge of contempt we feel when we see another person's lovely kitchen isn't about the kitchen. It's about discontent.

THE GRASS IS GREENER ON JOHN'S SIDE OF THE ROAD

The Bible talks extensively about contentment and its enemy: discontent—which happens to be close friends with envy: "And [Jesus] said to them, 'Take care, and be on your guard against all covetousness, for one's life does not consist in the abundance of his possessions'" (Luke 12:15).

Jesus' counsel in Luke 12 connects covetousness with an abundance of possessions. When we desire what others have, we reveal what our heart deems most valuable in that moment: things. And there are few places as susceptible to covetousness as the home.

The first home Josh and I owned was a small, 1940s cottage on a quiet downtown street. It had green shutters and a yellow door, two massive maple trees in the front yard, and a cracked sidewalk with crumbling steps. We loved it: every chipped part of the picket fence, the little brick patio, the galley kitchen where Josh built me a Julia Child pegboard. But the one thing we *didn't* like was the front yard. The grass was patchy and turned brown wherever the maple trees didn't cast shade. We raked and tended, fertilized and sowed. Nothing doing; grass wouldn't grow.

John's yard was across the street. As a teacher, John had all summer to tend his yard—and it showed. His grass was the color of the garden of Eden's, probably. Each morning when I went for my walk, his in-ground sprinklers came spinning up like otherworldly robots. Josh and I would stand at our living room window and watch John work. "It's honestly quite mesmerizing," Josh said. "His yard is . . . perfect."

"We're creepy." I laughed. "Isn't this the epitome of 'the grass is always greener'?"

We thought John's yard—sitting as it was across the road—highlighted the bleakness of ours. In light of John's grass, ours looked even more pathetic. That is, until I saw the yard on Rose Street. Turning the corner of the road, I came upon a scorched patch of grass, unrevivable even by the best of gardeners. It had been roasted by the July sun with no maple trees to help the cause. Cracked, brown, and utterly dead, the Rose Street yard made ours look like a golf course. *Perspective.* We were reminded, too, that our life stage was nothing like John's. In our season of little children and tight budgets, we couldn't devote the time necessary to have a flourishing front yard. John's was beautiful. Ours, not as much. But both were good in their own way.

Truthfully Josh and I coveted John's yard. His abundance made us conscious of our lack. But when we gained perspective about our yard, recognized our limitations, and appreciated the little we did have, we became conscious of the abundance right in front of us. Discontentment and envy blind us to the goodness of the home beneath our feet, the provision already in our hands. And the battle for Christians in today's society is to "keep [our] lives free from the love of money and be content with what [we] have, because God has said, 'Never will I leave you; never will I forsake you'" (Hebrews 13:5 NIV).

A STRONG FAITH IN GOD'S PROVISION

The author of Hebrews told us that the key to contentment is *a strong faith that God will take care of us.* We can be free of the love of money and be fully content in the homes we have when we are *confident* that God will not leave us. If we flip the argument, the author of Hebrews implied that envious, discontent people believe God is untrustworthy. When we choose discontentment, we're essentially saying: "What You've given me is not enough. I don't think You really love me. You won't take care of me, so I need to take care of myself." This kind of discontentment is often flanked by anxiety and urgency; a desperation to grasp the thing we believe will calm our roiling desires.

So when Black Friday sales offer up yet another perfect home, our anxious hearts become blind to God's provision.

If I only had a kitchen like that, I would have people over.

If I had a closet like that, I would feel confident in myself.

If I had a living room like that, I would take better care of my house.

Discontent always lives in the future, never in the present. It consumes every good thing and is unable to see the beauty right in front of it, chewing up the goodness but hungry for more. *If I had this, if I had that, if it were different* prevents *I'm so glad I have . . . , I'm so grateful for . . . , I'm living an answered prayer.* Discontentment is an insatiable beast, which is why it depends so much on envy; envy keeps it alive with a daily reminder of what is lacking. To kill discontent we must first kill envy. To do that, we must return to Hebrews 13:5: "Keep your lives free from the love of money and be content with what you have, *because God has said*, 'Never will I leave you; never will I forsake you'" (NIV, emphasis mine).

The author of Hebrews commanded us—in God's authority—to reject materialism and to choose contentment. But he does not do so arbitrarily. He told us we *can* obey these commands (he assumed our success) *because* God will never leave us. He was not saying to recite verses or tell ourselves God won't leave. He was saying: *God is not leaving you, and that is your present reality. Will you trust this is true or not?* Because God *will not* leave you or neglect you, you can choose contentment. You can trust God's heart for you. You can reject an urgency about money and status because God is *for you*.

You don't need the Instagram house to be loved by Him. The espresso machine is not evidence of more or less favor. More money, a nicer kitchen—these are not sinful. It is not wrong to be rich; it is not wrong to be poor. But it *is* wrong to place ourselves in God's rightful role as provider: Jehovah-jireh.

Discontentment destroys a good, beautiful, and true homelife. Only those whose eyes can see beauty in the most average, mundane places will find fulfillment in the regular days of home. This is why discontent is so evil. It robs us of eyes to see. It keeps us from seeing the ways God is already providing. It tells us our blessings aren't good enough. It isolates us, locks our doors, empties our table, and turns us self-centered—making us paranoid and insecure. Discontent is a liar, a robber, and a cheat, and God offers us a way out: faith. We can't move to a deeper, richer theology of home until we deal with this lack of trust in our hearts.

I often think about the homes Jesus entered during His ministry. Humble homes, wealthy homes. Accepted homes, unaccepted homes. Jesus displayed no favoritism when it came to the tables at which He dined. He dined with prostitutes (Luke 5:30), dishonest government officials (Luke 19:1–10), and members of the religious elite who would eventually have Him killed (Luke 11:37–54). Jesus did not hesitate to gather with people and speak truth and love, regardless of their financial status.

The apostles carried Jesus' example forward in their instructions to the New Testament believers. James wrote:

> My brothers, show no partiality as you hold the faith in our Lord Jesus Christ, the Lord of glory. For if a man wearing a gold ring and fine clothing comes into your assembly, and a poor man in shabby clothing also comes in, and if you pay attention to the one who wears the fine clothing and say, "You sit here in a good place," while you say to the poor man, "You stand over there," or, "Sit down at my feet," have you not then made distinctions among yourselves and become judges with evil thoughts? Listen, my beloved brothers, has not God chosen those who are poor in the world to be rich in faith and heirs of the kingdom, which he has promised to those who love him? (2:1–5)

We read this passage and cringe at the thought of rejecting someone due to their poverty. We would never invite a celebrity or wealthy businessman to have the best seat in church! Can you imagine if we made the poorer members of our congregations sit in the back or the balcony, with "reserved" front seats for the big tithers? We are quick to reject such distinctions and nod in agreement with James.

And yet, what we would never do to another person some of us do to *ourselves* every day. What we would never say about another person's home we say about *ours* every time we look around at the shabby walls. We pay attention to the wealthy, fancy, trendy homes. We celebrate them in media, Instagram, and Pinterest boards, but to our little oak dining table we say: "You stand over there." We look at our tiny living room and say: "This is no place for hospitality." The distinctions we would never apply to another person we apply daily in our words about ourselves and our homes. We have distinguished ourselves as the ones who must "stand over there" or "sit down at the feet," refusing to walk in the commission God gave us. We pay attention to what is rich and shiny but refuse to honor the blessings beneath us. Deep down, many of us believe ourselves and our homes unworthy in the eyes of God and His people. Rather than accepting God's love, we unconsciously try to prove ourselves through a perfectly clean or perfectly on-trend home (or both). This is wrong! When we judge God's gifts as lacking, or let discontent rule our hearts with lies, we are *unable to obey God*. If Jesus saw humble homes as worthy of His presence, worthy of good work, worthy of feasting, who are we to say they are not?

CONTENTMENT LEADS TO JOY

I met Lacey when Josh and I were first married. We lived in a Virginia apartment, second story. Looking back at pictures I chuckle at the rose-colored glasses of a new bride. The kitchen tiles looked perpetually dirty, there was no dining area to speak of, and we had to beg our landlord to use a bit of paint. But I felt so blessed!

Lacey and I became friends through an acquaintance, and I was excited to have her over—to begin my hosting journey as a young wife. But my expectations were dashed. Lacey was kind about our little apartment—but only insofar as it was compared to hers.

Our layout was better than hers.

Our furniture was nicer than hers (even though it was all secondhand).

Our kitchen was bigger than hers.

Our fireplace existed, and hers did not.

I found myself embarrassed to have her in my home. Everything about our apartment seemed to make her feel bad. Her backhanded, self-focused compliments made me feel like a problem; I was a constant reminder of what she didn't have. The joy I had when

Lacey walked in the door vanished into thin air with each jealous, comparative comment. Lacey's discontentment didn't just rob *her* of joy; it robbed me too.

If you're struggling to enjoy your home, discontent might be the offending party. As envy and covetousness increase, discontent increases too. We look around at what we don't have and can no longer see what we already possess. Discontent robs us of joy, and it follows that restoring contentment restores happiness at home.

Here are a few assessment questions for determining if discontentment may be behind your unhappiness in the home:

- Do you find yourself constantly comparing parts of your home to those of friends and family?
- Are you drawn to beautiful rooms on Pinterest/Instagram, not just for appreciation but out of a constant desire to change what you have?
- Do you feel anxiety or urgency to alter your home, or at least part of it?
- Do you feel jealous when someone renovates or decorates outside your budget?
- Do you find yourself complaining more than rejoicing?
- Do you have a hard time finding anything to like in your house?

If you answered yes to most of those questions, discontentment is the culprit! But here is the good news: discontent can be eradicated and joy can be restored. Joy at home, joy in the daily routines of dishes and laundry, joy in the morning and evening—it is all available! It's available in your imperfect, old, grubby, needs-some-TLC kitchen just as much as it's available in the subway-tiled renovation. Joy is here because Jesus is here, and He likes humble homes.

If you're ready to take back your joy, contentment is here to help: "Not that I am speaking of being in need, for I have learned in whatever situation I am to be content. I know how to be brought low, and I know how to abound. In any and every circumstance, I have learned the secret of facing plenty and hunger, abundance and need. I can do all things through him who strengthens me" (Philippians 4:11–13).

In context, Paul, writing to the church at Philippi, was talking about his recent sufferings. "I have learned in whatever situation to be content" referred to multiple beatings, imprisonments, and threats, things most of us aren't dealing with. When Paul said he knew the secret to contentment, we can trust him! In being brought low or experiencing abundance, contentment brings joy. But more than that, contentment brings strength.

That's right: the verse athletes love to write in their social media bio doesn't have anything to do with the big game. "I can do all things through him who strengthens me" is about contentment.

I can be fully content with an imperfect home through Him who strengthens me.

I can open my door confidently through Him who strengthens me.

I can fill my table with food and people through Him who strengthens me.

I can enjoy my daily tasks of dishes and mopping and laundry through Him who strengthens me.

And let me tell you, friend: the person who is truly content at home, willing to see God in the most mundane and humble of tasks? That person will see more of God with every passing day. Her contentment not only brings joy, it brings satisfaction, fulfillment, gratitude, and purpose. Discontent robs you of all these things.

THE STEWARD WHO LOST HIS WAY

In the much-loved fantasy series *The Lord of the Rings*, the throne of Gondor goes centuries without a king. As the city awaits the prophesied return of their king, a series of stewards guard the throne. Each steward cares for the city in the absence of the king, handing down his responsibilities to the son after him. As the years go by, the stewards forget the king is coming and become infatuated with their own power. In *The Return of the King*, Denethor, the current steward of Gondor, refuses to acknowledge the rise of Gondor's heir. Instead of handing over the throne, he misses the biggest moment in his city's history. He loses sight of the mission by losing awareness of the king.

Like Denethor, we are all stewards of a temporary city. All our belongings—home included—aren't really ours: "Every good gift and every perfect gift is from above, coming down from the Father of lights, with whom there is no variation or shadow due to change" (James 1:17). Everything we have was first found with God. Seeing our belongings as His *first* changes our perspective. We are not owners; we are stewards. In the gospel of Matthew, Jesus told a story about three servants entrusted to steward their master's money while he was away. To the first servant the master gave five bags of silver; to the second, two; and to the last, one. The first and second servants invested the money and doubled what their master had entrusted to them. But the third servant was afraid. Instead of using the master's money wisely, he buried it in the ground where no one could see.

The master was delighted with the first and second servants, responding: "Well done, my good and faithful servant. You have been faithful in handling this small amount, so now I will give you many more responsibilities. Let's celebrate together!" (25:23 NLT). But when he called the third servant forward, this man blamed the master for his own poor choices: "Master, I knew you were a harsh man, harvesting crops you didn't plant and gathering crops you didn't cultivate. I was afraid I would lose your money, so I hid it in the earth. Look, here is your money back" (vv. 24–25 NLT).

Perhaps you're wondering what the servant did wrong. He didn't lose the money; he returned it safely. The master had much to say:

> "You wicked and lazy servant! If you knew I harvested crops I didn't plant and gathered crops I didn't cultivate, why didn't you deposit my money in the bank? At least I could have gotten some interest on it."
>
> Then he ordered, "Take the money from this servant, and give it to the one with the ten bags of silver. To those who use well what they are given, even more will be given, and they will have an abundance. But from those who do nothing, even what little they have will be taken away." (vv. 26–29 NLT)

The context of this parable is the stewardship of the gospel—the revealed Word given to us, to be shared and multiplied, not hidden from view. If we believe that God is a hard and judgmental master, withholding what we really want or deserve, we will bury the gifts He's given in the dirt of discontent. Our eyes focus only on the lack, and what could have been multiplied rots away in the dark.

What if we chose to live like the first and second servants? What if we embraced the little and used well what we were given? If we don't care for the home we have now, we won't have the habits and heart to care for a bigger one. If we don't see the home we have as good enough, as worthy of our work and attention, how will we steward God's blessings when they are bigger? We are shaped by the seasons of smallness. Our ability to be content in the dirty-tile kitchen and the tiny living room or busy schedule shapes our character if, or when, our dreams come true. Henry Blackaby wrote in his famous book *Experiencing God*: "If you can't be faithful in a little, God will not give you the larger assignment. He may want to adjust your character through small assignments in order to prepare you for larger ones."[1]

In my very first apartment I shared a three-bedroom flat with two other girls. I had several roommates over those years and quickly learned that good roommate relations don't happen by accident. Each person had to pull her weight. When I didn't do my share of dishes, they piled up in the sink and affected other people. When I didn't care for the shared bathroom, my roommate experienced the effects. The "little" of my first apartment was an opportunity to be faithful and diligent, skills I would need when I married Josh and we had an apartment of our own.

When I moved in with Josh after our wedding, I learned how to care for our hand-me-down furniture, tiny kitchen, and balcony garden. Once again: faithfulness with little prepared me for the larger assignments later to come, like the garden I now plant with my three children, or the cleaning routine I manage for the five members of our family. If I had waited to learn necessary skills because I wasn't in the season I wished to be, I wouldn't have the skills I needed for the season I'm now in.

Like Denethor, we tend to forget we are the stewards and instead assume we are the kings. *We deserve better. We deserve more.* We see God as a threat, a withholding master, rather than the Father of lights who gives us every good gift (James 1:17). True stewardship knows the limits. Good stewards make the most of where they are, whether their station changes or not.

RESTORING OUR JOY

God's provision, and our reliance upon it, brings contentment and restores our joy. Recognizing that we are not owners but stewards should encourage us to be faithful with the precious little God has given, knowing that our faithfulness with what is small builds character for greater stewardship down the road. This is nitty-gritty. It's as practical as making the effort to care for the hand-me-down furniture, setting up a cleaning routine for your week, and doing the dishes after each meal so they don't pile up for your spouse or roommate. Stewardship grows diligence, patience, and a grateful heart. These attributes are gifts in themselves, but they also grant a lovely side benefit: the ability to love the home you have.

That's what contentment is, really. Learning to love the goodness in what you've been given rather than striving for more and better. Contentment doesn't end our dreaming or dash our hopes; it simply looks with grateful eyes on the beauty *already here*.

Loving the home you have is an act of defiance against discontent, and there are some practical ways you can move toward a grateful, observant heart.

ASK: IS THIS UNDER MY CONTROL, OR NOT?

The side entrance to our downtown cottage had three doors. It was a nightmare for bringing in groceries: the outer door, which opened to the right, led to the basement door, which opened to the left, but up the steps was the kitchen door, which opened into the other two doors. In the winter the outer door would get blocked with snow and stop opening completely. There was no access between the narrow, old garage and the breezeway.

I abhorred that entry (if I thought I could lose my salvation, I would have lost it myriad times coming through those three doors!). But changing the entry would require a complete renovation of the kitchen, basement stairs, and garage access. It was not in our budget and therefore out of my control.

When I accepted that the door situation would not change—it was completely out of my control—I came to peace with it. Even though it still frustrated me at times, I found things to be grateful for: less cold air crept into the kitchen with the three blockades; the breezeway was convenient in winter; we had a nice entrance to the kitchen.

Our front entry was also in need of improvement. The front

door opened into a three-by-three foot entry with a tiny coat closet. With the number of people we hosted each week it was far from ideal. We couldn't renovate it, but there were other things under my control. We made a large piece of driftwood into a coatrack and attached it to the wall. We put boot mats on the wooden floor beneath it, moving people out of the tiny entry and into the living area. A space that used to irk me became beautiful!

Loving the home you have is about releasing control of the things you *just can't change* and taking charge of the things you *can*. Maybe you can't afford a brand-new sofa, but maybe you can afford new throw pillow covers and a few pretty blankets, even from the thrift store. Instead of shrugging your shoulders and saying, "I just can't have nice things," take control of what you can. Create some beauty! Thrift a beautiful new art piece for the bedroom wall and rearrange it to make a haven of peace. Declutter your kitchen cabinets and hang a tea towel on the stove. Paint a wall, plant some flowers, move the couch to a different corner. There is something you can do now, something under your control, that you can change to love your home more. Do not wait for some future day to enjoy the blessing beneath your feet.

REFLECT: AM I ACTING IN GRATITUDE OR AM I FEEDING MY ENVY?

Our behaviors reveal our hearts. When we find ourselves continually drawn to envy, discontentment, and criticism (of others or ourselves), we must turn inward and ask the question: *Is this gratitude or envy?* Just asking the question usually reveals the answer! As convicting as it is, we know God is gracious for our failures and will restore our hearts.

To this day, most of my home is thrifted, but even thrift finds can be the product of envy. I saw a beautiful playroom on Pinterest and wanted to replicate it on a budget, but I was infuriated by the constant state of my kids' playroom (I seem to have forgotten it is a *play*room, not a *museum* room). I was hunting thrift stores for cute macramé art pieces, big floor baskets, and other Pinteresty things. The bill was adding up. I had to stop and ask: *Is this desire for a perfect playroom really for my kids, or is my own idealism and envy driving this?* By pointing out my sinful push for more, the Lord helped me grow content with the imperfect, messy, but well-loved room.

POUR OUT: DO I SEE MY HOUSE AS MOSTLY FOR *ME* OR FOR THE SERVICE OF GOD AND OTHERS?

Do our homes really belong to us? No! Our homes first belong to God. He is the center, the cornerstone, the foundation of everything. A space to live is a precious gift and a home is made within it. Making a home isn't about collecting stuff; it's about *forming people.* As we discussed in the first chapter, some homes form us negatively. Biblical homes form us lovingly. But they can only do this if the home is built on a precedent of selflessness.

When we view our homes selfishly and self-protectively, we inevitably experience isolation. Community and hospitality go hand in hand. An open door and open hearts are unified in mission. If we wish to go deeper with people, if we wish to grow in love and grace, we must see our homes as built for more than just our own leisure.

This doesn't mean you have people in your home every night of the week. Let's not go to extremes. It means you have an open-handed posture with the house God has lent you. Like the stewards in the parable of the talents, we do not actually own everything we have. It first belongs to the Master, the lover of our souls. When we understand our possessions as gifts from God—the owner of all things, without limit in His abundance—it's easier to share them with others. How can you use this space to bless someone, even just one person? This begins with the ones who live there of course, but it does not stay there. Who can you invite for pizza? How can you use this space, imperfect or small as it may be, to bring someone else joy?

When you look at your home as a vessel of love and safety, you may find your own joy increase as well.

CHECK THE HEART: DO MY SOCIAL MEDIA AND SPENDING HABITS FEED CONTENTMENT OR MATERIALISM?

Lastly, our social media and spending habits should be checked against the gratitude meter. Social media is a marketing engine; yes, we use it to connect with friends, but we also use it to find products we like (hence social media influencers) and to peruse the latest trends and shop the best deals. When we consume more than we create, scroll more than we innovate, we can easily be trapped by a materialistic mindset (even if the money stays in our wallet).

Do you need a social media break? Do you need an Etsy, Pinterest, or HGTV break? Whatever is feeding your discontentment should be set aside for a period of time. Some call this "fasting," a time of restraint during which you focus on prayer and spiritual disciplines. Historically, fasts were from food, but fasting from other things we believe ourselves dependent upon can expose areas we didn't realize God desired to work on.

Loving the home you have is a process. Look around your space and count five things you're grateful for, and then ask yourself: *How can I live contentedly in this space, since God believes this is where I belong for now?* Are the things you dislike under your control or not? If they are, how can you create beauty here?

God has given each of us a little something—a little corner of a house or perhaps a large and sprawling abode. Whatever He has given is meant to be loved and stewarded well, then shared with others so they can experience His goodness too. As we live out a content, grateful posture, we often find that the things we thought so ugly, so inconvenient, and so subpar have worked a change in us that a perfect kitchen never could have accomplished.

Maybe the home you have is the kind Jesus would have liked to visit. Can you love it, just as it is?

> But godliness with contentment is great gain, for we brought nothing into the world, and we cannot take anything out of the world. But if we have food and clothing, with these we will be content. (1 Timothy 6:6–8)

CHAPTER 3

Creating a Culture of Faith

A list, crumpled and coffee-stained, lies
next to the lunch dishes half-checked;
a census of hours spent on obscure
tasks, boomeranging back in the whir
of weekdays. "Do you get weary of it,
the repeating mundanity?"
I don't.
Is it that lists are proof I've lived something good
in those hours—not the "good" of Instagram,
but the good of open-mouth baby kisses and
lisping questions and crooked J's? Or maybe
it's the smell of rising dough and rush of
     outside cold,
the scrolling purr of scooter wheels, the flicker
of fireplace and candle flame, the tinny ping
of piano keys? They are all there, every day,
on the list. Yet they are new, as if it were
first step, kiss, loaf, lisp, candle, song.
       "The List," *PDM*

FROM AGE FIFTEEN TO AGE TWENTY-FIVE I WAS JUG-gling school and work. Except for a brief one-year break, those ten years were filled with college-level homework as well as part-time and full-time jobs. When I got married at almost twenty-four, I had a full-time job I loved: admissions adviser for my collegiate alma mater. Helping students figure out their career track, strate-gizing transfer credits, and walking through scholarship options with families brought me so much joy. When Josh and I found out we were pregnant with our first child on our one-year anniversary, I was traveling around the US to conference centers, high schools, and homeschool groups to talk about the college process. I didn't plan to quit my job after the baby was born, but I hoped to shift from office work to a remote position.

Up to this point, my spiritual life had dovetailed into my busy work life smoothly. I would get up early, go to the gym, grab cof-fee, and study my Bible before work. If I couldn't get to it in the morning, I would spend time studying and praying on my lunch break. I assumed that my spiritual disciplines, which had always fit so neatly into my busy life of school and work, would not change once I had kids and worked from home. How much could one baby change?

Adeline was born during a whirlwind move from Virginia to Pennsylvania. It was then I realized I could not continue my remote position. I sadly resigned the job I had held and loved for almost five years. This was an excruciating decision, since I loved my job and did not want to leave. For the first time in ten years, I was neither working nor in school. When Josh returned to work five days after Addie was born, I stood in an empty house, holding my newborn baby, baffled by how much time I had on my hands. The linoleum was cold on my bare feet and I thought: *I can't remember the last time I was barefoot in my own house. I'm usually out the door in heels by now.*

I entered a new season, and at first, it was sweet. I loved the slow pace of tending the baby, reading books, and going for walks. But one thing I did not anticipate was the effect leaving work would have on my spiritual life.

Before the baby I equated a strong spiritual life with an hour in the Word of God each morning. I had a solid routine that worked for me, and even when it didn't work the way I planned, I could always make time for God later in the day. But with a new baby, my mornings didn't look the same. Sometimes she woke up five times during the night and in the morning I staggered downstairs groggy-eyed. Other times her morning nap was short and I couldn't study as long as I wanted. I tried reading the Bible while nursing in my chair, but between fountains of spit-up and the balancing act of a Bible on the chair arm, side table, and sofa cushion, I gave up that idea too. In truth, I needed the Word—and I knew it. I was questioning my season, looking for the purpose my work had given me. I had led a very disciplined, structured life, but the discipline and structure were imposed *upon* me by a syllabus or supervisor. Now it was up to *me alone* to intentionally create discipline and pursue the spiritual life I thought I'd lost.

THE SPIRITUAL DISCIPLINE OF HOME

The word *discipline* comes from the Latin root *discipulus,* which means pupil or student.[1] To "discipline" is to teach—we know this from the study of parenting. But we often forget the application of discipline to *ourselves.* When we pursue spiritual discipline, we teach ourselves rhythms that spill over into every area of life. Unfortunately, many of us feel like I did in my transition to motherhood. When seasons change, when we lose external structure, or when we simply need to create structure for ourselves, we flounder or fail to follow through. And when days turn to weeks turn to years without any kind of spiritual rhythm, faith becomes nothing more than the title for a vague belief system. It no longer transforms our lives.

What does this have to do with home? *Everything.* One of the biggest roadblocks to a life of spiritual discipline is a feeling of chaos and overwhelm. And one of the biggest *blessings* of spiritual discipline is its positive impact on every area of life: home, work, relationships, and physical health. On home, because spiritual discipline leads us to see mundane tasks as an act of worship. In work, because we learn how to let Christ shape our purpose rather than finding identity in what we do. In relationships, spiritual discipline grounds us in Christ's unmoving love so we do not rely on humans for fulfillment. And in physical health, because the disciplines of a strong spiritual life lead us to habits of rest and restraint that benefit our bodies and are supported by science. And spiritual discipline—learning how to prioritize intimacy with God—begins at home. It does not begin in a church building or a Bible study group. And only when we recognize the *need* for spiritual discipline do we create the rhythms of home necessary to sustain it. The home supports our spiritual life, and our spiritual life creates a safe, connected, and welcoming home. As we walk out our faith daily, we become more like Christ: a safe place to land, deeply connected to God and others, fulfilled by His goodness.

My discontent leaving the workplace happened largely because I had formed my identity around production. My work was my worth and my worth was found in work. My spirituality was centered on rhythms imposed upon me by the structure of a corporate workplace or university class schedule. When those things were removed from the routine, I had to completely reconstruct my understanding of my purpose. Before my resignation, I found purpose by being successful, efficient, and moving up the ladder. I had clear benchmarks and external validation for achieving them. Now no one saw the work I did; no one celebrated finished dishes or folded laundry or changed diapers. Nor was there any external structure to enforce discipline and follow-through, spiritually or otherwise. Standing in an empty duplex kitchen with a one-month-old, I could choose to see my home as "in the way" of a fulfilled, purposeful life, or I could choose to see it as *the way itself*. I chose the latter, and it changed the trajectory of my home and family.

It all started with a Bible study basket. I put all my Bible study supplies—a journal, Bible, pens, commentary, and sticky notes—into a thrifted basket in the middle of the dining room table. Josh left for work at 6:00 a.m. and I got up to feed the baby. Those first few months I'd feed her at the table, holding her with one arm and writing with the other. My season was new. I felt wobbly in my purpose. But I figured, if I made the discipline of seeking God as convenient as possible, I would follow through . . . and I did. I made it as easy as possible for the season I was in. And then that small act of discipline *multiplied*.

With no one around to give me a syllabus or a work schedule, I made my own. Before the baby, I still had to do housework, but there was less of it and I could usually finish it over the weekend. Josh and I both traveled extensively for work, so our apartment stayed almost completely clean. Now that I was home alone with the baby, without the pressure of top-down deadlines, it was up to me to create order and purpose in the unseen tasks I now handled.

I divided the laundry across days of the week. I divided up the cleaning too—so I wouldn't have to do it all in one day. I created a rhythm of outings with the baby coordinated to her feeding patterns. And slowly, slowly, the feeling of confusion faded. Home was no longer a place to escape; it became the place I wanted to be.

Through the discipline of Bible study in that season I learned discipline in other areas as well: my physical fitness improved because I knew when to push through and when to give myself grace. I got better at budgeting for our meals and cooking from scratch, something I'd had less time to figure out when I was traveling for work. And even though I was still blogging and writing, I wasn't doing it to prove something to myself or others; I was doing it for the joy. The spiritual discipline of Bible study led to a greater ability to sit with silence, to be in solitude, to push myself to do hard things. Through this spiritual formation my home itself was formed and a culture of faith, a place of strength and safety, was born.

CULTIVATING A CULTURE OF FAITH

When you hear "culture of faith" your mind might immediately turn to child discipleship—parenting children. But a faithful home culture applies to *all* Christians. You don't have to be a parent to create a home culture founded on faith. While parents have a unique and important role in discipleship at home, single and childless Christians do too. Single Christians are some of the best candidates for developing a deeply formed homelife.

I recently asked the single and empty-nester members of my Instagram audience to share how they have cultivated a culture of faith in their homes. Here are a few of their responses:

- becoming a place for travelers to stay
- hosting social functions

- being open for late-night conversations
- inviting people over for meals
- cleaning the space and creating a calm place of welcome
- seeking out non-Christians and inviting them in as friends
- mentoring teen girls
- hosting a backyard picnic for neighbors
- putting Scripture throughout the home to remind myself of God's truth
- hosting Bible studies

These are things people can do in any season of life, but the single and empty-nester Christians noted it was far easier for them to stay up late, host with no regard for bedtimes, and use their freedom for the sake of the gospel than it might be for parents of young children. And as I learned in my working years, the structure of my generally free life provided opportunity to serve others. Childless people may be busier in some ways, but freer in others.

Which brings me to the most important truth: the spiritually disciplined home life is, in itself, freedom. We think of discipline as rigid, limiting, keeping us from something. But discipline does not just restrain; discipline *sets free*. When we live without boundaries, we constantly experience the unwanted consequences of our actions. These consequences have the power to keep us from the freedom of a life of peace, joy, and fulfillment. If I choose not to care for my home all week, I might lose an entire Saturday cleaning it up. If I choose to live reactively instead of implementing a gracious structure, I might experience a constant state of stress. If I choose to idolize the opinions of people instead of prioritizing my time with God, I might never open my door to let people in. *Undisciplined* people experience the most bondage—bondage to stress, overwhelm, fear, and chaos.

Discipline trains us to press through what is uncomfortable for the prize on the other side. Sometimes the prize is intimacy with

God (such as in the discipline of Bible study and prayer), but other times the prize is something seemingly less spiritual. The spiritual discipline of home provides many such "prizes":

- the prize of *joy* when you look at a home that is furnished with your own delight and taste in beauty (without being materialistic or financially irresponsible);
- the prize of *peace* when you end the day without overwhelm;
- the prize of *self-control* when you reject the culture's demand for bigger, better, and fancier;
- the prize of *community* when your rhythms make hospitality natural and easy; and
- the prize of *satisfaction*, knowing you showed up well in your home and are an effective worker within it.

There are countless more rewards to the spiritually disciplined life at home. These rhythms are inherently fulfilling. Yet because so many of us did not have parents who passed down (1) a strong faith culture and (2) home management skills, it's easy to feel lost in the quest for freedom. We will get into the very practical application of discipline in the chapters on home management itself, but before we do, let's look more at the heart behind a culture of faith and why it matters so much for us today.

THE HOME IS WHERE THE HEART IS

In 1 Corinthians 3 the apostle Paul told us: "According to the grace of God given to me, like a skilled master builder I laid a foundation, and someone else is building upon it. Let each one take care how he builds upon it" (v. 10). In context Paul was speaking of discipleship: the slow build of faith on the cornerstone of Christ, the foundation on which we build our lives (v. 11). This cornerstone for faith was predicted by the prophet Isaiah: "Therefore thus says the Lord GOD, 'Behold, I am the one who has laid as a foundation in Zion, a stone, a tested stone, a precious cornerstone, of a sure foundation: "Whoever believes will not be in haste"'" (28:16).

Christ is our tested and precious cornerstone—unwavering, unchanging, and stable in all His ways. When built on Him, our homes are founded on all things good and true. Our belief in Him does not return void! Whether single, married, parenting littles, or seeing your littles off to college, your home will be a haven if it is based on the goodness of God. But we must *take care* how we build on God's foundation. It is possible to have a home originally founded on Christ, a culture that bears His name but does not bear His fruit:

> If anyone builds on this foundation using gold, silver, costly stones, wood, hay or straw, their work will be shown for what it is, because the Day will bring it to light. It will be revealed with fire, and the fire will test the quality of each person's work. If what has been built survives, the builder will receive a reward. If it is burned up, the builder will suffer loss but yet will be saved—even though only as one escaping through the flames. (1 Corinthians 3:12–15 NIV)

How we build the culture of our home—the place where we are our truest spiritual selves—will one day be shown for what it is. Anyone who has experienced hypocrisy or spiritual abuse can attest to the painful ramifications of the Christian facade. A truly Christ-centered home doesn't pursue righteousness to impress others or host company to show off the house. We don't decorate the walls with Hobby Lobby signage without also changing the interior of our hearts. A culture of faith is created when the hearts of those within the home are fixed on Christ Himself. Out of this heart transformation, we pursue the disciplines of the spiritually strong life—not to impress or show off or prove anything (to God or people) but to experience the richness of communion with God and man.

When motherhood changed my life, I had no idea how much of my identity relied on my work. My discontent was not the fault of the home; there was plenty to do and plenty to challenge me. My discontent was the result of a long-term addiction to achievement and externally imposed structure. I thought the only things worth doing were the things people could see and applaud. The only work worth improving at was instantly measurable or beneficial to *me*. Idolatry of work cannot coexist with a strong theology of home. When we view the home through God's eyes, seeing it as a valuable, worthy, formative place, we gain much-needed perspective on what happens outside its walls. A home culture of faith sees *all* work as God's work, paid or unpaid. Laundry, dishes, cooking food, inviting people over, scrubbing floors—all of it glorifies God.

> Idolatry of work cannot coexist with a strong theology of home.

Until I recognized my desire to be *seen* was greater than my desire to be faithful, I resisted the season and God's call. Being home exposed my heart.

The old saying "home is where the heart is" is biblically true. At home, we are our truest, rawest selves. Our hearts are on display. Do our homes portray a heart dedicated to the truth of God? Is the culture of our safest place truly safe and good?

Those of you who grew up without a safe and good home—I see you. Your effort to break the chain of unhealthy home rhythms and unsafe home cultures will never return void, and God is your cheerleader every step of the way. You have a new foundation and you are a new creation! And through the spiritual discipline of home, you have the opportunity to build on that foundation the "gold, silver, costly stones" of the Holy Spirit. The trials of life will test your building with fire and it will be refined into something far more beautiful than you ever imagined.

Home is where the heart is . . . and the heart is formed at home. The culture of faith we build through spiritual discipline turns around and blesses us with a newfound freedom. As we discipline ourselves to seek God, to make time for Him, we begin to see the home as a place of purpose. And when we see the home as a work worthy of our time, attention, and effort, we find ourselves less burdened by the place we live and *freer* to pursue the abundant life God offers. This is the beautiful cycle of the disciplined life, a theology of home—returning to the garden the only way we can: by building on the foundation of Christ.

> By wisdom a house is built,
> and by understanding it is established;
> by knowledge the rooms are filled
> with all precious and pleasant riches.
> (Proverbs 24:3–4)

CHAPTER 4

Restoring the Foundations

The rage builds red,
churning hot;
the mirror holds the face of his father.
Fists clenched, he closes his eyes and
exchanges seething for strength.
The blond boy, the one always with him,
sees the surrender,
and another link
is broken.

The day goes down
a thrashing wreck,
the plan neither peace nor perfection.
Heart benched, she closes her eyes and
exchanges screaming for strength.
The dark-eyed girl, the one in the car seat,
hears the "Help me,"
and another link
is broken.

The dawn comes early,
casting beams
across the pages lying marked and messy.
Not yet dressed, she closes her eyes and

exchanges insecurity for strength.
The little ones, the ones always watching,
feel the faith here
and another link
is broken.

This enslaving anger,
guilt
and unfaithfulness,
cynicism,
criticism,
condescension,
contempt—
link by link drop powerless as children choose
faith and hope,
love and peace,
restraint and grace.
And after days of this choosing
become years of the same,
the grandchildren no longer know
the slavery of their forefathers
because someone loved them . . .
enough to break the chain.

"To Break a Chain," *PDM*

MY GREAT-GRANDFATHER RAN AWAY FROM A DETROIT orphanage when he was eleven years old.

Cheslov Durczynski knew he couldn't stay in the orphanage where he and his sisters were forced to live. After all, Cheslov was not an orphan. He was only in the orphanage because his mother had died and his father was an alcoholic.

So little Cheslov ran away. Winding his way out of downtown Detroit, he made it into rural Michigan and worked on a farm to survive. Years later he returned to the city, found a job as an assistant at Sunnyside Bakery, and made his way up the ranks. Eventually he bought the bakery and built a successful business. My grandfather, Gerald, grew up benefiting from the beautiful cakes and pastries Chester Duran—no longer Cheslov Durczynski—created: tall, spiraling wedding cakes and delicious sugary desserts.

I grew up fascinated by Great-Grandpa Chester's story. It was inspiring, challenging, harrowing. My siblings and I sought more information to fill in the gaps, but Grandpa Chester's line ended at his alcoholic father. We couldn't find any information beyond records of a Polish mining company and my great-great-grandfather's immigration documents. In contrast, my husband can trace his heritage all the way back to the founder of Pennsylvania, William Penn. I suppose you could say I have "genealogical jealousy." In my father's line, there is little family identity to latch onto and Grandpa Chester didn't even want to keep the same name as his father. There isn't much history to build on. The family tree just kind of . . . ends.

Maybe you look at your family tree and see the same ending. Some of our family trees don't bear good fruit. Some of them have dark and twisted branches, and others are bent and broken. Some fruit is rotten, while some never grew. How do you build a sense of identity when the home you come from isn't a pattern with which you want to identify? How do you form a view of home that aligns with God's when it feels like *everything* is against you?

Perhaps you haven't asked those questions, but you've felt them in your heart. Your family line is littered with the wreckage of bad decisions and broken relationships. You are reflecting on the eternal purpose of the home and its tasks, but your mind can't let go of the ugliness home has been. Your family line is so intertwined with your view of home, they're almost inseparable. And that makes sense. Family and home are integrally connected. Our identities are shaped in the spaces we live. Studies have found that unhealthy, chaotic home environments can even have a lasting impact on our health.[1] Our experience of the physical home affects us more profoundly than we realize, down to our sense of security, purpose, and identity. Many of us desire to know where we came from so we can know where we are going. The unstated longing within us is to belong, to have a legacy. Not just a legacy we leave behind, but one that came before.

A LEGACY FOR THE LEGACY-LESS

The Bible speaks to our desire for an identity, for a history, for a family tree. The gospel of Jesus Christ offers a legacy to the legacy-less, an identity to the lost, and a family for those who are alone. Christianity is not an invitation to an individual pursuit of God (though that is part of it). It is an invitation to join a collective gathering of believers. We are not meant to follow Christ in isolation! We become one family with all the children of God: "So we, though many, are one body in Christ, and individually members one of another" (Romans 12:5).

For our family's morning time (snacks and read-alouds) I'm currently reading the original *The Pilgrim's Progress* to my girls.[2] *The Pilgrim's Progress* is an allegorical tale of a traveler named Christian, who leaves the City of Destruction to follow Christ. My girls love the story: the adventure and allegory resonate with them. And as much as I appreciate it, I have one disagreement: Christian walks most of the path of faith *alone*. It works for the analogy John Bunyan was going for, but this solitary pursuit of the Celestial City is not what Romans 12 describes! The Christian life is not a lonely walk uphill toward God. It is simultaneously an adoption, an initiation, and an inheritance.

ADOPTION

To become a Christian is to be adopted into the family of God. No matter how broken our human families, we have a place in the family of God. We are called children (John 1:12), sons and daughters (Romans 8:15 NASB), and heirs of God (Galatians 4:5–7). This is not a solitary adoption either. We are not God's "only" child! When we join the family of God by allegiance to Christ, we join thousands of others who are equally loved by God: our siblings in the faith.

INITIATION

Because we are entering a family, we're also gaining a family history. To be a Christian is to be initiated into an existing legacy—one that is two thousand years old! We're not only joined on the journey by living saints, we're following in the steps of the saints who went before us. *Saint* simply means "set apart one" and is the name for anyone who follows after Christ (the apostles greeted Christians as "the saints" in their letters). We can learn from the Christians who came before us, our foremothers and forefathers in the faith. Missionaries, pastors, apostles, prophets, theologians, and martyrs inspire us to live authentic lives for Christ. We are part of their legacy and continue that legacy into the future.

INHERITANCE

Galatians 4 tells us that we are "heirs of God." We inherit all the benefits and rights a daughter of God deserves—no matter what we have done. Christ has made us clean and given us a new identity! With that identity comes inheritance (Ephesians 1:11–14; Colossians 3:23–24).

If *The Pilgrim's Progress* were biblically accurate, Christian would be walking the road arm in arm with hundreds of other pilgrims, bolstered by their respective gifts. And he wouldn't be walking blindly: the footprints of the pilgrims who walked before him, the faithful Christians of centuries past, would mark the way of Christ for Christian to follow.

Our experience of the Christian life today, however, looks a lot more like *The Pilgrim's Progress* than Romans 12. Most Christians don't know their legacy because most churches don't teach church history. Some Christians don't even value the church—the body of believers—for the community it is (or should be). Without a strong sense of spiritual family, connection to our legacy, and an eye to our inheritance, it is no surprise Western Christians feel rootless and alone in faith, especially when building a culture of faith at home. We've forgotten our legacy. And recovering that legacy doesn't begin in a church building; it begins with the rhythms of faith at home.

RECOVERING A LOST LEGACY

The chains of our *physical* family legacy are broken by the *spiritual* family legacy we have inherited through Christ. The consequences and implications are not erased; we still live in a fallen world being sanctified by the Holy Spirit. We must still allow the Lord to free us from unhealthy patterns, sometimes through the practical helps of counseling, science, and sociology. But this freedom begins with acknowledging our new identity. We are not chained to the past. We are not destined to repeat it. Christ is making all things new, not just in heaven but here and now: "I remain confident of this: I will see the goodness of the LORD in the land of the living" (Psalm 27:13 NIV). Not the land of the dead, not the land of the resurrected; no, the goodness of the Lord will be visible *in the land of the living* and in the places people live: at home.

You might still be wondering: *What exactly is the story I'm born into? What is my Christian legacy and how does that impact my home?* I'm glad you asked! *Our legacy is a generational vision based on the lasting values of the Christian faith.* These values are things like:

- Compassion (Ephesians 4:32): We empathize with the wounds of others that we may usher them toward true healing.
- Benevolence (Galatians 6:10): We seek the best interest and good of others at every opportunity; we do all the good we can.
- Generosity (Luke 6:38): We hold our belongings loosely, willing and ready to share with others because Christ has shared everything with us.
- Forgiveness (Mark 11:25): Because we have been forgiven much, we forgive others.
- Hospitality (Hebrews 13:2): We open our homes not just to friends but to strangers and those who lack community and affection.

- Humility (Proverbs 22:4): We reject pride and conceit, choosing to see ourselves as people loved by God, and outdo one another in showing honor.
- Justice (Isaiah 1:17): We seek to do what is right and just because God is righteous and the author of justice.
- Peacemaking (Matthew 5:9): We do not keep the peace by avoiding conflict but make peace the way God does.
- Mercy (Luke 6:36): Because we are under the mercy of Christ, we are quick to show mercy to others.
- Purity (1 Timothy 4:12): We pursue lives of holiness, rejecting sin and becoming more like Christ in purity so our actions no longer hurt us and those we influence.
- Repentance (2 Peter 3:9): We repent quickly when we have done wrong, knowing we have forgiveness in Christ, making right our offenses toward His people.
- Wisdom (James 1:5): We revere God so our minds are guided by His wisdom, asking Him to make up for our limited view of the world.

We could easily add to this list the fruits of walking by the Holy Spirit (Galatians 5) and Romans 12:9–21:

Love must be sincere. Hate what is evil; cling to what is good. Be devoted to one another in love. Honor one another above yourselves. Never be lacking in zeal, but keep your spiritual fervor, serving the Lord. Be joyful in hope, patient in affliction, faithful in prayer. Share with the Lord's people who are in need. Practice hospitality.

Bless those who persecute you; bless and do not curse. Rejoice with those who rejoice; mourn with those who mourn. Live in harmony with one another. Do not be proud, but be willing to associate with people of low position. Do not be conceited.

Do not repay anyone evil for evil. Be careful to do what is

right in the eyes of everyone. If it is possible, as far as it depends on you, live at peace with everyone. Do not take revenge, my dear friends, but leave room for God's wrath, for it is written: "It is mine to avenge; I will repay," says the Lord. On the contrary:

> "If your enemy is hungry, feed him;
>   if he is thirsty, give him something to drink.
> In doing this, you will heap burning coals on his head."

Do not be overcome by evil, but overcome evil with good. (NIV)

If we were to distill the idea of Christian legacy into a single line, it would be Romans 12:21: "Do not be overcome by evil, but overcome evil with good." Christians are handed a victorious legacy. The apostle John wrote in 1 John 2:14: "I write to you, young men, because you are strong, and the word of God lives in you, and *you have overcome* the evil one" (NIV, emphasis mine). In Revelation 2–4, Jesus told John through a series of visions that the "victor" (believer who endures in her faith) will receive specific blessings and rewards from God. He was not referring to our salvation here; our salvation is secured through the cross and resurrection of Christ. He was referring instead to the fruit of a faithful, enduring, overcoming life. This is the life of a Christian who overcomes evil, not by studying evil and its movements but by embodying what is good.

A home foundation built on Christ is such an active attack against evil. This home is not passive. It is not checked out about spiritual things. It is a vibrant, thriving center of discipleship, built on what is true, good, and beautiful. It is a safe place for people to know and be known. It may be small and humble, but its impact is eternal. Those who view their homes (and the breaking of generational chains within them) as the work of God are overcoming evil with good; by walking in the Spirit of God and producing His fruit, they take an offensive position against the evils of our present age. Victorious living, enduring love, and the good fight of faith begin at home.

Your lost legacy was recovered at the cross. And now—we build upon it.

BREAKING GENERATIONAL CHAINS

When I think about my grandpa leaving the orphanage at eleven years old, the mother in me wants to weep. *Eleven? That's the same age as my friend's son. Barely older than Adeline.* I picture his spindly legs and wide, boyish eyes and wonder: *Did he escape at night? Did he hide in a Hamtramck alley and eat scraps from trash cans as he wound his way out of downtown Detroit?* My heart breaks for a boy left an orphan. A boy without a home.

Perhaps that's why Jesus' words in John 14:18 resonate so deeply: "I will not leave you as orphans; I will come to you." Not only will Jesus father those with no family (or no family to emulate), *He will come to them.* Like the father in the story of the Prodigal Son, Jesus doesn't settle for welcoming us back; He runs to meet us. "He settles the childless woman in her home as a happy mother of children. Praise the LORD" (Psalm 113:9 NIV). Jesus hands a legacy, an identity, a home culture to anyone who calls upon His name.

I don't have the time, space, or expertise to fully address the tangled web of dysfunctional family relationships, child trauma, socioeconomic inequality, physical housing difficulties, and myriad other factors contributing to our negative experiences of home. These are the heartbreaking consequences of a broken, sinful world. I have seen and experienced some of these consequences firsthand. They are not easily overcome, and I would never indicate otherwise.

There are authors wiser than me who have written practical books addressing these specific issues, but this book must stay true to its intent: to show the way to a Christian theology of home, the foundation underpinning all practical "fixes" the world has to offer. The counsel of child development professionals, licensed professional counselors, educators, sociologists, historians, and scientists is helpful and important. But without a strong theology of home, a sense of Christian legacy and vision (who we are and where we are going), practical tips will be Band-Aids on a broken bone. Or rather, a broken home:

- If I know my three-year-old needs my comfort and attention during a breakdown, but I am drowning in housework and overstimulated by my own space, I may struggle to parent him well. *I am missing a theology of stewardship.*
- If I can only afford a small apartment, but I feel embarrassed of my financial limitations and unwilling to have people over for dinner or coffee, I may feel perpetually isolated and lonely. *I am missing a theology of hospitality.*
- If I am suffocating in my dark, cluttered, dirty space, to the point my mental health is struggling, but don't have the tools to know how to clean (or how it would help me), I may feel trapped in my own house. *I am missing a theology of diligence.*
- If I need more nutritious food for my mental and physical well-being, but I was never taught to cook or prioritize learning how, I may struggle with my mood, body image, and energy levels. *I need a theology of the body and food.*

Theology simply means the study of God: who He is and how He interacts with the world. A theology of home—and the stewardship, hospitality, diligence, and food within it—is simply God's perspective and heart for how His children experience homelife. Without understanding God's heart for the home, we will Band-Aid the visible issues but will never truly *heal.*

Oh, friend, how I wish I could tell you more of my own family story. I know it would bring you great hope: hope that the brokenness of home you may have experienced can also be reversed and healed. Though I cannot share the details of the pain my parents walked through and the redemption we've experienced in our family line, I can share something my mother said when I talked to her about building a new foundation from the rubble of past generations:

The reasons we even have to build a new thing on the actual truth is because falseness and decay destroy generations. When one's guard is dropped, when the truth is traded, when men and women live for self rather than God and others . . . [there are consequences]. For me, it was as if a bright light was shining when I heard the Bible or read it. It was so nourishing and pure. There was no doubt, right to and through to my soul. And I had lived a young life with so much doubt . . . I am a living, breathing testimony to God that He will not forget even one.

My parents recovered a lost legacy and I, in turn, benefited from that faith. They staked their lives and home upon the unchanging goodness of God and His gospel and it changed a generation. It changed a family line. And this living God can do the same for you.

I will restore the fortunes of my people Israel, and they shall rebuild the ruined cities and inhabit them; they shall plant vineyards and drink their wine, and they shall make gardens and eat their fruit. (Amos 9:14)

CHAPTER 5

The Spiritual Rhythms of Home

I read the words that Luther wrote:
"So much to do, I'll spend three hours
in prayer." I shrink and turn
to a calendar scoured for space—
I'm doing much, do I have three hours?
Should I *make* three hours?
Scratch it out between bacon and bedtime,
get up at four before the babies do?

I see the words that Tozer wrote:
"The man who would truly know God
must give time to Him," and I think:
I haven't much time to give. These hands
are held by disciples who don't tithe,
who walk on toddler legs. Is divided time
still time that counts?

But I know the words that Jesus said:
a welcome for the little and the lost.
This Shepherd-King who gently leads
those with young—He understands
divided time. The prayer split triple,

whispered by a stove, a sink, a blacked-out
    nursery, is liturgy too;
full hands worship
as well as empty ones.

We are the daughters of Katharina
and Susanna, Perpetua and Lydia
who would not delay devotion
for some future day,
some noiseless morning,
to meet the God of unquiet
whose Temple is a kitchen floor.
This time is a seen and sacred hour
and I will not wish away their childhood
as if Christ is put off
by the bleating of His lambs.
      "THIS SEEN AND SACRED HOUR," *PDM*

My husband and I are both second-generation home educators. If you're not familiar with home education, it's not as simple as "school-at-home." There are a variety of educational philosophies homeschoolers choose from; in our home, we follow a classical model blended with the teachings of a nineteenth-century schoolteacher named Charlotte Mason.

Mason believed children are "born persons," as in, they are born with a whole personality and inherent value that should be honored in their education. This led her to an education model based on "living books" (books that teach through story and beautiful writing, as opposed to dry textbooks), lots of time outdoors, hands-on activities, and interest-led learning. In the other model, classical education, students learn how to memorize information, connect patterns and ideas, and then debate and critically think through those ideas in community.[1]

In both the classical and Charlotte Mason philosophies, students learn they are part of a bigger story. The literature they consume, the ideas they are exposed to, and the living history they are invited to participate in teach them facts beyond the textbook page. It is easier to remember because it's interesting; easier to enjoy because it's alive! In this context, history, science, and language aren't disconnected subjects. They are woven together into a living, breathing story, one in which the student fully participates.

Christians often treat spirituality the way schools treat subjects: separate classes. Over here, the daily life class; and over there, the religion class. Our faith and daily tasks are seen as separate, divisible entities with little crossover: *I finish my devotions and then do the dishes*. We've trained ourselves (or been trained by culture) to separate real life from real spirituality, to divide physical homelife from Christian legacy. But the consequences are dire. The Bible becomes a textbook: memorize, recite, regurgitate. Our prayer times become request lists. Our faith is something jammed in as an afterthought rather than the center from which we live and move and breathe.

Charlotte Mason believed education could be a joy. By connecting with the larger story of the world, focusing on the truth, goodness, and beauty within it, she helped students love learning. I believe our spirituality could use a dose of Charlotte's vision. So many of us are disconnected from the larger story (our legacy), no longer living from the strength of identity found within the gospel. We might *live* our faith, but we don't *love* it. It feels dry, boring, and dutiful. It's something we do, not something we enjoy; it is a source of accomplishment, not affection. Or perhaps it's the same routine we followed as children, an empty ritual devoid of joy. And when that is the case, very little truth, goodness, and beauty echo within our homes. We feel it. We know it. But we feel helpless to fix it.

The thing we feel helpless to fix is our *home culture*. Perhaps it feels like too great a task, we're tired, or we don't know where to begin. This culture exists whether you're single in an apartment or married with eight kids in a suburban sprawl. The dictionary defines *culture* as "the customs, arts, social institutions, and achievements of a particular nation, people, or other social group."[2] I would add "priorities" to that list. Your home culture is made up of the specific *customs, arts, social commitments, priorities, and achievements* of yourself and those who live with you. For Christians, these five elements should be driven by our legacy of faith. Our Christian legacy guides the mission and priorities of home, and therefore the culture of it.

I'm not suggesting every tradition, hobby, or social commitment should be explicitly Christian. To the contrary, a truly Christian home culture will be engaged with the world and seeking the welfare of the city in which it resides (Jeremiah 29:7). I am suggesting that our Christian identity should translate to life lived at home *more* than it currently does. Our customs, arts, social commitments, priorities, and achievements should reflect this identity. As we live into an embodied faith, we find greater fulfillment in the repetitive, daily tasks of home, as do the people who come to our doors. Charlotte taught children to love learning, and this same model of *embodied story* can lead us to love our faith. When you not only love God but love following Him, even the home reflects your affection.

Building a home on the affection of God will not happen by accident; it takes intention. But we do not need another spiritual checkbox; we need spiritual rhythms. Lucky for us, we have inherited these rhythms with our Christian legacy through something called the *church calendar.*

RHYTHMS OF FAITH, EVERY DAY

If you were asked to list the Christian holidays, you'd probably start with Christmas and Easter. Depending on the church you were raised in (or lack thereof!) the list might end there! Protestant Christians in America usually celebrate only these two. Liturgical churches (such as Catholic, Orthodox, Anglican, and Lutheran) celebrate more than these, and their calendars differ slightly.

The church calendar is a lived liturgy, a pattern of worship woven into the seasons, not added onto an existing life but acting instead as the foundation for living. You might be wondering what a liturgy is, so let me explain. In a church setting, *liturgy* can describe the direction for how a Christian service should be held—an order of events directing worshipers toward God through Communion, public Scripture reading, hymns or songs, and other rituals. All churches still possess a form of liturgy. But liturgy is more than just the order of service. Rod Dreher describes it this way in his book *The Benedict Option*:

> All of life is liturgical, in the sense that all our actions frame our experiences and train our desires to particular ends. Every day we are living out what [James K. A. Smith] calls "cultural liturgies" of one kind or another. . . . Christian liturgies, on the other hand, should lead us to desire communion with God. The basis for our liturgies is the one who unites the medium and the message of the Gospel: Jesus Christ. . . . Liturgy is primarily, though not exclusively, about what God has to say to us.[3]

Liturgy is not something trapped within a church building; it is the pattern, the expected trajectory, of Christian life.

In this sense liturgy is not something trapped within a church building; it is the pattern, the expected trajectory, of Christian life. God "speaks" through the physical elements of bread and wine, the action of kneeling in prayer, the call to communal singing, and the "awe-filled meaning of . . . sacred moment[s]."[4] For the Christian, all moments are sanctified by the presence of the Holy Spirit. Our sacred moments are not limited to Sundays; they are just as present when washing dishes after work on a Monday night.

Our days themselves are liturgical—physical reminders of the spiritual reality. Liturgy is not just for church. It is not just empty ritual. It is not just for worship services. Liturgies are woven into every day of our lives as Christian people. Each movement of our day can turn our eyes toward Jesus. In liturgical church settings we might sit, kneel, stand, sing, or pray during set times of the service. And during our daily tasks we sit, kneel, stand, scrub, and move—all opportunities to sing, pray, meditate, worship, and allow our actions to direct us into reverence for God. Yes, even our most mundane tasks can be liturgical acts.

Liturgy is more sacred moments, though. Liturgy can be woven into the very fabric of our schedule: the days that turn to weeks that turn to months have a recognizable rhythm. Most evangelical Christians acknowledge some of these rhythms in the form of Easter and Christmas, but there is more to it than these two holidays.

This is where the church calendar comes in. Christian holidays act as signposts to the sacred nature of time. It's not just December 12; it's the season of Advent. It's not just a gloomy March day; it's Lent. The period between the great seasons of lament (Lent and Advent) and celebration (Christmas and Easter) is called Ordinary Time. *Ordinary* simply means "counted." Ordinary Time is a season for commemorating the themes of salvation history, and yet it is called *ordinary*. For thirty-three weeks, the church calendar hums quietly between Easter (March or April) and All Saints' Day (November 1). For thirty-three weeks Ordinary Time passes on, but the ordinary is also sacred. Just like the Christian life.

I did not grow up celebrating the church calendar. I grew up in the Pentecostal/charismatic tradition and my parents later moved to Baptist or nondenominational settings, so the only Christian holidays we celebrated were Christmas and Easter. In the Baptist settings (and the Baptist college I attended), the church calendar got some side-eye. Skeptics saw it as the trappings of "dead religion," an empty ritual no longer necessary to Christian life. This fear of liturgy and ritual is not completely unfounded; many Protestants have experience with hollow liturgical settings where ritual has indeed replaced a living relationship with Christ. But the ritual itself is not the problem, spiritual deadness is. When rhythms of faith are paired with hearts who seek the kingdom, there is no dead religion.

When I attended a Presbyterian church in college, and later, Anglican, Catholic, and Orthodox services, I was amazed at the depth of history and experience available in the church calendar. Though my husband and I are not in a liturgical tradition (we have been in half a dozen denominations together over the years and are currently nondenominational), our family follows the Lutheran church calendar. The calendar anchors us. It grants a gentle rhythm pointing us toward Christ: an opportunity to rejoice, remember, return, and rebuild.

THE PURPOSE OF THE CHURCH CALENDAR

Observing the holidays that are part of our Christian history is not meant to be a burden. In fact, in some traditions, the church calendar has been modified to avoid this. When Martin Luther separated from the Roman Catholic Church, one of the things he altered was the Catholic church calendar, which at the time was burdened with hundreds of saints' days, fasts, and ritual requirements. Luther's calendar celebrated the saints' days of the apostles and Old Testament believers. It observes Lent, Easter, All Saints' Day, All Hallows' Eve, Advent, Christmas, and Epiphany, among a few other special days. These days are not added onto our personal calendars as "extra work" but as reminders of the faithfulness of God in everyday life. Church holidays are an opportunity to live out four *R*s.

REJOICE

In the Old Testament, Israel was given festivals to celebrate the goodness of God. These celebrations were an opportunity to rejoice communally for the provision they received. As the church in the first century transitioned from mostly Jewish to mostly Gentile, these festivals took on the messianic overtures of Christian celebration. Passover became *Pascha* (which we know as Easter in English-speaking countries but which remains a form of *Pascha* in most other languages). Pentecost (*Shavuot*) stayed Pentecost, but with a new focus on the giving of the Spirit instead of the giving of Mosaic law. Christians rejoiced together during Advent to celebrate the second coming of Christ. Christmas (Christ's Mass) was a ceremony looking forward to the great day of His return, eventually changing to celebrate His first coming—in Bethlehem—as well. Holidays were and are for rejoicing! They are moments in our calendar to celebrate the goodness of God.

REMEMBER

Church holidays are also a time to remember. Lent is a great example of a "remembering" holiday. So is Advent. During these seasons we can recall the faithfulness of God. Early Christians did a lot of remembering: they were much more connected to the apostles, aware of their teachings and passing them down to the next generation. They remembered through scriptural teaching and gathering, of course, but the church calendar played a role as well. It's hard to forget the story you're a part of when the calendar itself reminds you!

RETURN

During seasons like Lent, we are convicted to return to Christ's way. We lament where we have walked away from God, repent of the things keeping us from free fellowship with Him, and return to a deeper intimacy and faith. Seasons like Lent and Advent, when

71

we expectantly look forward to celebrations of Christ's birth or resurrection, remind us of our daily need for God. They keep us from only focusing on the peaks of faith and not the valleys.

REBUILD

The church calendar also offers an opportunity to rebuild, or to build again, what has been torn down in our life, faith, or family. We can rebuild traditions, integrating more richness, beauty, and love. We can rebuild rhythms, following the calendar year with grace instead of striving. We can rebuild family culture, pushing back against a chaotic or abusive upbringing with patterns of peace and grace. The church calendar gives us a chance to build something new or rebuild something broken.

If you're new to the church calendar, you might be wondering where to start! I definitely don't recommend biting off more than you can chew. It can be as simple as beginning with the existing popular holidays of Easter and Christmas, integrating a stronger Christ-focus into each of them. You don't have to do it all! A little bit, gradually over time, is better than changing everything at once. Remember: the church calendar is *your* legacy. How you choose to celebrate it is customizable to your season of life.

In my (very busy) season of littles, we celebrate the major holidays and a few mainline saints' days, as you'll see below:

St. Valentine's Day (February 14)
St. Patrick's Day (March 17)
Lent (the forty days leading up to Easter)
Easter/Resurrection Day (varied)
Pentecost (the fifty days after Easter)
Ordinary Time (weeks between Pentecost and Advent)
All Hallows' Eve (October 31)
All Saints' Day (November 1)
St. Nicholas's Day (December 6)

Advent (the four Sundays before Christmas)
Christmas Day (December 25)
Epiphany (January 6)

This is not the full calendar (we could do more!), but the spacing of these days works well with our schedule. They add a gentle rhythm of celebration to our year without overwhelming or burdening us with must-dos.

What's the point of celebrating? Other than the basic idea of rejoice, remember, return, and rebuild, it's a way to connect with our Christian legacy. We read books and stories about the people of faith before us: Valentine, who performed marriages for Christian Roman soldiers; Patrick, who brought the gospel to Ireland; the disciples, who preached the gospel to Jerusalem at Pentecost; and of course Jesus Himself, the epicenter of Christmas and Easter!

There are endless resources we can use to study these people, to learn from them and their faith, to imitate Christ and see our days centered on the rhythms of His reality. And this is not something we do alone! During the larger Christian holidays we can and should celebrate with our spiritual family, the church. But we also invite friends into the Christian holidays because this faith is not meant to be walked alone! Our annual All Saints' Day party, hosted on Halloween, is one of our favorite traditions. We pack the house full of food and friends (including over a dozen kids), and sing hymns, play games, eat "saint cupcakes," and spend time interceding in prayer for our city.

We have discovered that this legacy of faith can be deep and joyful, rich and free. There is no dead religion here. There is Christ.

We are not meant to be spiritual orphans, winding our way through life on a pilgrimage all alone. We walk in the steps of the saints who came before us and become better saints ourselves by doing so. We need the saints of our cities—fellow believers—to walk with us. And we need saints of the past—Christians of great character—to learn from. Between them both, we find a family. With the legacy given to us, we find a rhythm. And in all of it, we find a home.

This is the day that the Lord has made; let us rejoice and be glad in it. (Psalm 118:24)

CHAPTER 6

All to the Glory of God

Quiet my heart and I'll hear at last
the thrumming love makes when pause lets
    us rest.
Still my soul and I'll see through the haze
the myriad ways You loved me
before I was able to open
the eyes of my heart to behold them.
I was afraid to see You;
all the glory and wrath they told me about.
But now I have heard and have seen;
I opened my eyes by faith in Your goodness
and to my joy and surprise
You were actually good.

    "SHOW ME YOUR GLORY," *PDM*

GRANDMA—THE SAME GRANDMA OF ROAST BEEF AND Maxwell House coffee—taught me how to mop a floor by hand. I never saw my grandma mop a floor any other way. It was the way it was: on hands and knees with a washcloth, a butter knife for the cracks between the floorboards, and a bucket of increasingly dirty water. It was a dreaded task when I was a child, but even twelve-year-old me could recognize (and take pride in) the beauty in the gleaming wood. Grandma would heave a sigh as she clambered to her feet and tossed the filthy water out the door.

"Cleanliness is next to godliness!" she'd say.

"I don't think that's in the Bible, Grandma," her know-it-all grandkids retorted.

"Well, you can't complain about a clean floor," she huffed back. And she was right.

Fast-forward twenty years, and I didn't do a good job of handing down her mopping skills. I excused myself due to a leg injury that made kneeling on the hardwood difficult. When my oldest was eight years old she saw me mop on my knees for the first time. She watched with wide eyes, then said: "How nice that mops were invented in my lifetime so we don't have to do that anymore!" If only she knew!

In Adeline's eyes it was impractical to mop a floor on hands and knees when a perfectly good stick mop sat in the closet. But truth is, I missed Grandma's method. You see more clearly on your knees; you catch the dirt you'd miss if you were standing up. The slow back and forth of washcloth on wood takes longer, even takes more effort, but results in a cleaner floor. Does it really matter which method I use? In the grander scheme of things, probably not. Though Grandma's view of cleanliness wasn't biblical, her belief that unseen tasks deserve to be done well . . . *is*.

Grandma believed in hard work for hard work's sake. Scripture talks about hard work too, but for a much deeper reason. In his letter to the Corinthian church, the apostle Paul spent considerable time teaching the Corinthians how to love God well. In 1 Corinthians 10, he spoke about the importance of loving God by loving others. He commanded the Corinthian Christians not to put a cause of stumbling in the way of a weaker brother, to be willing to lay down their preferences and freedoms to encourage holiness in someone else. He concluded this section with a simple summary: "So, whether you eat or drink, or whatever you do, do all to the glory of God" (v. 31). In other words, commentator Matthew Henry writes, "In eating and drinking, and in all we do, we should aim at the glory of God, at pleasing and honouring him. This is the fundamental principle of practical godliness."[1] The natural product of a Christ-transformed heart is godliness, and a godliness pervading everything we do—including our daily routines.

Our daily routines contain some of the most repetitive, mundane, unseen things we do. This is where we are most likely to take shortcuts, to choose the easier route. And sometimes the easier route is the better choice for the season, but like Grandma said: *"You can't complain about a clean floor."* There is something satisfying about tending a home with excellence, not because people see you but because *God gave a gift* and you wish to glorify Him with it. David Guzik wrote on 1 Corinthians 10:31, "The purpose of our lives isn't to see how much we can get away with and still be Christians; rather, it is to glorify God."[2] But what does it mean to glorify God? What does it mean to glorify God in the mundane work of mopping floors, when no one is there to see the difference or no one notices but you?

The word *glory* in Hebrew means "weight," and to attribute glory to God is to give *honor* or *weight* (significance, reverence) to Him. In Exodus 33, Moses asked to see God's glory and God replied, "I will make all my *goodness* pass before you" (v. 19, emphasis mine). To glorify God is to attribute honor to Him, to point people to Him, and to exalt His goodness in the eyes of the world. So how do we do this through something as simple as the daily routines of home?

One answer is found in another epistle of Paul, this one to the church at Colossae: "Whatever you do, in word or deed, do everything in the name of the Lord Jesus, giving thanks to God the Father through him. . . . Whatever you do, work heartily, as for the Lord and not for men" (Colossians 3:17, 23).

These two verses are found about a paragraph apart in Paul's letter. I've placed them together for ease of comparison. In the first line, Paul told us that everything—word and deed—is done in the name (authority) of Jesus and is worthy of thanksgiving. This includes the labor of every daily task! Remember, Paul wrote this encouragement to people who didn't have dishwashers, powerful vehicles, and handheld computers at their fingertips. What we call mundane, boring, and repetitive would have been life-saving to people walking to work in physically laborious jobs, making every meal from scratch, and mending their own clothes. To Paul (and to God), the unseen necessary tasks of home are not unimportant. They are an act of worship. They bring glory to God.

Which brings me to the second verse. In verse 23, Paul told

us to "work heartily, as for the Lord and not for men." In context, Paul was talking to *servants* and *slaves*. The culture of Paul's day depended in part on slave labor and indentured servanthood. The jobs these Christians held were necessary for survival, but they were *not* freely chosen. Yet Paul told them to *work heartily*, not out of obligation, resentment, or duty but out of love for a heavenly Master; one who loves and sees their work.

Most of us are not tending to a home as indentured servants, but at times we may still feel a measure of obligation, resentment, and duty. Paul's command to servants applies to us. Will we work heartily at home out of love for our Father, the giver of all good gifts? Or will we continue to look at the work of the home as an obligation—a dirty, necessary duty to be tolerated and endured? This is not the attitude of a Christian worker. Perhaps we need a better theology of work.

CORRECTING OUR THEOLOGY
OF WORK AT HOME

In my childhood home we cleaned the kitchen after dinner each night (a big job since we fed eight people). The job wasn't done until the counters and sinks were wiped down, a gleaming Formica space clear of the last bits of dinner; another rhythm passed down from grandma to son to mother, something all of us kids were trained to know. Dad called it "a complete job,"—being thorough, committing to excellence in unseen places. And as children tend to do . . . *we hated it.*

"Who *cares* about clean counters?!" we wailed each weekday night.

When I was sixteen—with many years of wiped counters and sinks under my belt—my dad called me to his office. "Check this out," he said. He pointed to a black and white photo: a smiling, middle-aged woman leaning on a stainless-steel counter. "She's the manager of the Dairy Queen," he said. I leaned closer.

"So?"

"Look at what she says about the sinks." He stabbed one calloused finger at the tiny print. "*I wipe down the sink every evening,*" the paper read. "*It's so satisfying to see it shine. I know no one cares, but I do.*"

"This is a woman who takes pride in her work," Dad said, closing the paper.

"Did you pay her to say this?" I said, teenage eye roll included.

"I know you kids make fun of me for the sinks," Dad said with a laugh. "But one day you'll think like this woman"—he nodded toward the paper, which was now on the floor—"And you'll see that a job well done is satisfying in itself."

Take pleasure in your toil. Perhaps Dad was right? Even in a fallen, broken world, it's possible to not just do the work of home well but to enjoy it. Part of the joy is in getting better at it, learning the skill of it. As we become better at the care of home, it turns around and grants us happiness. I think this is because work—the tending, gentle work of home—*is the very first work that existed*. It's the work of God.

"The LORD God took the man and put him in the garden of Eden to work it and keep it" (Genesis 2:15). Genesis 2 is the chapter *before* the fall of man. It depicts the perfection of the garden: a place of peace and unity, a place of beauty. Also, a place of work. That's right: *work is not a product of the fall*. When Adam and Eve sinned against God, God initiated a curse on the earth and the serpent. Both of these, he promised, would one day be destroyed. As a consequence of this curse—the natural outworking of sin in the world—the man and woman would be affected in terms of their primary labor. The man would labor with difficulty in the ground. The woman would labor with difficulty in her fertility. Both would feel the *pain* (same Hebrew word as *labor*) of the other's burden, and both would be affected by the impact of sin.

Work, which was a joy and a blessing before the fall, became a burden after it.

Work is not bad. Work is good. God is a worker (Genesis 1–2), but unlike humans, He knows when and how to rest (even though He doesn't need it). There is no reason to think heaven will preclude working; if it existed in the first creation, it will likely exist in the second!

I argue that because God is a worker, because work is good and preceded the fall, work is *still good* and it is possible to "take pleasure in our toil"—including, or especially, in the home. We resent the repetitive nature of it, but what if the repetition is exactly what we need? We despise the dirtiness of it, but what if this selflessness is the shaping of our character? We hate that it is unseen and uncelebrated, but what if this hiddenness is teaching us humility?

Perhaps, like mopping a floor, the spiritual discipline of home is seen more clearly on your knees. You catch the dirt you'd miss if you were standing.

SIX MINDSET SHIFTS TO TAKE PLEASURE IN YOUR TOIL

I did not accept my father's admonition to enjoy gleaming sinks, not for many years. I may be proof of the long-term effects of parenting, but it was not until I owned a home of my own and automatically went through the motions previously taught that I realized the *benefit* of working at home. What I hated as a teenager came back to bless me as an adult. These skills served as a foundation for what I continued to learn about loving my home and the work it takes to tend it.

Some of you reading this book did not have a father who commended clean sinks. You may be the very first person in your family to believe the home worthy of good work, and you are not alone in your diligence! *God sees.* It is God, the one who sees in secret, who rewards you. It's really not about the sinks and floors at all; it's about stewarding God's gifts in God's joy.

If you're used to caring about work only if it is measurable, seen, or propelling you up a ladder, then working at home is a mindset shift. To go from seeing the home as a place to flop to seeing it as a place of purpose and worthy of effort (and consequently, a lovely place to flop as well!), we must reframe how we see our work and ourselves. My journey to loving the home was helped along by the spiritual disciplines I was taught as a child, but I had to learn other disciplines the hard way. Here are six mindset shifts that helped me remember *all* of life is to the glory of God.

I AM NOT UNSEEN; I AM SEEN.

Author Sara Hagerty wrote, "The craving to be seen is universal: we were made to be known. But there is only one who can know us. He is the one who created us to live with moments and hours that no one else can understand."[3] This is perhaps the most difficult part of enjoying the home: we must live in moments and hours no one else can understand, tasks no one else can do, work no one else will finish. We are unseen, unmeasured, uncelebrated. Sometimes it feels like no one cares if you unloaded the dishwasher; it just has to be done.

But what feels unseen and unimportant is seen and valued. If all work matters to God, and God Himself is a worker, it follows that the simple tasks of our everyday life matter to Him. His glory—His goodness—is displayed, sometimes imperceptibly, in the movements of our work. People might not see the work of tending a home as worthy, but God certainly does. Everything done with a heart of faithfulness is a worthy offering to our Lord: even dishes and laundry.

I AM NOT JUST CLEANING; I AM CREATING.

What if we saw these repetitive, uninteresting tasks as opportunities to create something beautiful? To make something new?

You might be thinking: *There is nothing new in this old apartment!* And that may be true. But chances are there's a new way to view it. There's a new way the old floor could look. There's a newness to work well-done, order created out of disorder. When we clean, tend, mend, and care for the places we've been given, we're echoing God's creative nature: "In the beginning God created the heavens and the earth. Now the earth was formless and empty, darkness was over the surface of the deep, and the Spirit of God was hovering over the waters. And God said, 'Let there be light,' and there was light" (Genesis 1:1–3 NIV).

Disorder to order. Chaos to beauty. The first chapter of Genesis depicts the big picture of creation: first God forms His world (days one through three), then He fills it (days four through six). Our homes are already formed, but they need filling. They need beautification and order. As image bearers of God, we have the honor of creating order where there is disorder; not a militant, inflexible order that turns a home into a museum but a lived-in order leading to peace. The most peaceful homes I've been in have been created with love and intention, thoughtfully arranged to welcome people in. There might have been some toys on the floor and dishes on the counter, but the overall sense in the home was order, not chaos. Rhythm, not impulse. A sense of calm and rest. *Form, then fill, then rest*: a rhythm of creation.

I AM NOT JUST WORKING; I AM SERVING.

The work of the home must be done, but why? Ultimately we work at home as an act of service to those living there (including ourselves). We do the dishes so we have spoons at dinnertime. We clean the bathroom so we can shower in a sanitary environment. We mend clothes so we can wear them longer. The work of the home might not be glamorous, but it is *important*; it blesses everyone it touches. By seeing our home rhythms as an act of service, we move outside ourselves to a selfless point of view.

Galatians 5:13–14 says, "For you were called to freedom, brothers. Only do not use your freedom as an opportunity for the flesh, but through love serve one another. For the whole law is fulfilled in one word: 'You shall love your neighbor as yourself.'" We certainly have the freedom to resist the work of home. There are days I simply do not want to care for the space in which I live. But in those moments, I must consider someone other than myself. I might be free to forget the work; I'm not being paid and I have no boss watching over my shoulder. But if the work of the home is a means of serving others, it takes on great value. I'm not *just* cooking dinner; I'm giving my time to those in need of food. The work of the home is an act of love for our closest neighbors: those who live within our walls.

We aren't alone in our unseen, selfless service: "Even as the Son of Man came not to be served but to serve, and to give his life as a ransom for many" (Matthew 20:28). The home is a place of rest, beauty, purpose, and, yes, service. With each tiny task we have the opportunity to bless others.

MY WORK IS NOT POINTLESS; MY WORK IS VALUABLE.

In this vein, our work in the home is not without value. Because it is seen by God, a reflection of His creative nature, and an act of service, the tending tasks of home bear incredible value. Maybe no one is checking your work to see that you did, in fact, vacuum behind the toilet or make the living room comfortable for guests . . . *but God saw.* God sees our effort, our diligence, and our attention to detail. He sees us stewarding His good gifts and sharing them with others. He sees and values what we do. To me, that's a reward in itself.

MY WORK IS NOT BORING; IT IS BUILDING.

If you ever want to rush past the mundane work to get to the good stuff, I hear you! Procrastination is my love language. If I can skip the hard parts and just do what's fun, I will do it every time. But I've learned that mundane work builds consistency, discipline, character, and—quite frankly—a life well lived. The comfort of waking up to a calm home, unimpeded by stacks of dishes and things I've put off to morning, is made available to me by building a habit of diligence. In other words: I bless my future self by doing boring things. Each time I choose to do the unglamorous, faithful task God entrusted to me, I choose a future blessing. Sometimes that blessing is as simple as waking up to less work. Other times it's more significant: like seeing my tolerance for hard things increase, or noticing beauty in places I ignored before.

Aimless choices lead to future stress. But when we look at the boring work as building work, we begin to shape a home that comforts, holds, and welcomes us. And when we feel comforted by our home, we are far more likely to open it to others, as God asks us to do (Hebrews 13:2; 1 Peter 4:9; Romans 12:13)!

THIS LIFE IS NOT REPETITIVE; IT IS RESTORATIVE.

Last but certainly not least: a purposeful homelife is naturally restorative. Many of us look at our homes as a place to collapse. The work of home is seen as an impediment to such leisure—we *have to* clean; we *have to* cook; we *have to* . . . But with life-giving routines, the necessary tasks of home don't take away energy; they bestow it.

A life, while full of necessary tasks, brings joy, clarity, beauty, and purpose *through* those tasks. Instead of escaping your life to find depth, you find it every day, three times a day, at the kitchen sink. Instead of wishing for the next vacation and hiding from the looming to-dos, your everyday routines become a time of sacred goodness, an experience of God's heart. The Shepherd of our souls meets us in the middle of the life we're given, granting us green pastures and still waters in the midst of mundanity. He restores our souls in the middle places, not just the mountaintops. I think it's no mistake God restores us in the places we most need restoring.

When we crave rest and wish for more than what we have, we're offered restoration, not by escaping life but by truly living it.

Shifting our mindset about home, its purpose, and the everyday routines we take for granted can be a difficult process. Have grace for yourself as you consider the ways you've thought about home before. It's never too late to make a change. There is hope for joy in joyless tasks, hope for goodness in boring places, hope for a life well-lived in the unseen moments. The spiritual discipline of home is a practice in the glory of God: a glory made visible by humble hands in humble places.

> I perceived that there is nothing better for them than to be joyful and to do good as long as they live; also that everyone should eat and drink and take pleasure in all his toil—this is God's gift to man. (Ecclesiastes. 3:12–13)

PART II

A Liturgy of Home

CHAPTER 7

Pearls Slipping Off a String

The Liturgy of Homemaking

MY FRIEND NAOMI WORKED THE NIGHT SHIFT AS A MATER-
nity nurse. Her hours were painful: start work at 7:00 p.m. and get
off at 7:00 a.m. Sleep took up the morning and any social time was
crammed into afternoons or right when she got off work; but many
of her friends were working a nine-to-five. As a single woman with
a shifting nighttime schedule, Naomi's life could not have been
more different from mine. But even in the midst of this busyness,
Naomi's home was a place of peace.

After climbing steep stairs to her second-story apartment, the
door swung open to a cozy kitchen. The space was stuffed with a
vintage dining table covered with a tablecloth and an assortment
of mugs and spoons. Her counters held what her cupboards could
not, organized in little jars and quaint stacks. The teapot puffed
happily on her stove and the living room was full of houseplants,
books, blankets, and thrifted furniture. It was the epitome of cozy,
welcoming, and calm.

On paper the demands of Naomi's life made calm seem inaccessible. But the rhythms of her home proved otherwise. Even during
stress and a demanding job, Naomi shaped the place she lived with

care and intention. She could have crashed after work (and I am sure she sometimes did), but she saw the care of her home as a means of restoration and created rhythms that sustained her on the hardest days. Incredibly, the rhythms she created blessed more than herself! When I was a young mom with a baby, visiting Naomi's apartment was always a respite—mostly because of her but also because she practiced a *liturgy of home.*

In the last chapter I talked about six mindset shifts to seeing home as a place of purpose. The final mindset is the most important: learning that a thriving home life is not just repetitive but innately *restorative.* We can't deny that home tasks are repetitive; they repeat every week, sometimes every day. But these repeated tasks, when understood through a lens of sacred purpose, restore to us the joy of our salvation (Psalm 51:12). Like the church liturgies that facilitate worship and meditation, the everyday routines of home can move us to adoration. These tasks, done day in and day out, can become patterns of worship in Christian life.

The famous redheaded heroine Anne of Green Gables had an appreciation for her home that outruns the rest of us. In the pages of the Anne series we meet a girl who sees beauty everywhere she turns: the apple trees, the neighbor's pond, the grassy fields, and the old farmhouse all receive new, glamorous names to reflect the intensity of Anne's adoration. In the second book of the series, Anne tells her adopted mother, Marilla: "I believe the nicest and sweetest days are not those on which anything very splendid or wonderful or exciting happens but just those that bring simple little pleasures, following one another softly, like pearls slipping off a string."[1]

How many of us wake up waiting for the splendid or exciting, overlooking the little pleasures God provides? I wonder if our eyes are so attuned to the dramatic that we don't have vision for the goodness of what is small. Our home tasks are not grand or exciting, but they are meaningful; they care for us and others.

They require us every day and shape our character by unseen increments. Tish Harrison Warren said in her book *Liturgy of the Ordinary*, "What we need is to learn a way of being-in-the-world that transforms us, day by day, by the rhythms of repentance and faith."[2] Anne had a way of being in the world that transformed her. She let the little beauties of daily life become, in themselves, exciting. We pass on our streets, the tasks of home always there like the scenery, beckoning us to be in the world in a humble, regular way. And if we let them, they can teach us faith. They teach us to rely on God for purpose, to create with Him a vision for beauty, and to see the humble things our hands mend, tend, and build as a place for people to be safe.

As a reminder, liturgy is a physical action leading to communion with God. Liturgies remind us of spiritual realities using earthly things. Our daily tasks act as liturgies by pointing our hearts toward worship, which is more than a church service. Through liturgies of the home, we experience a deeper intimacy with God because these daily acts are a form of worship:

> All worship is in some sense liturgical, but liturgies that are sacramental both reflect Christ's presence in the divine order and embody it in a concrete form accessible to worshipers. Liturgy is not magic, of course, but if it is intended and received sacramentally, it awakens the sense that worshipers are communing with the eternal, transcendent realm through the ritual and its elements. The liturgy feeds the sacramental imagination, reweaving the connection between body and spirit.[3]

Cleaning a home is not sacramental. But it can be liturgical: it awakens a sense that we are communing with the eternal. The God who sees our labor, who thinks it matters, and who rewards the unseen task is as present in our cleaning as He is in church. There is a holiness and humility in the liturgy of home; we are on

> There is a holiness and humility in the liturgy of home; we are on our knees more here than anywhere else. What if we met God while there?

our knees more here than anywhere else. What if we met God while there? Every action of our daily tasks is an opportunity to know God on a deeper level. Not a *single* daily task is a waste! But learning to see God in the liturgy of home starts by forming habits, or spiritual disciplines, within that home.

ROUTINES THAT RESTORE: SPIRITUAL DISCIPLINES OF HOME

We are back to that word: *discipline.* Don't shy away from it. Discipline, when chosen freely out of a desire to experience God's abundant grace, leads to *freedom.* We could even say discipline is a fruit of the Spirit (self-control, Galatians 5:23)! Disciplining our homelife means bringing the daily tasks and routines of home under the Spirit's leading. Scripture tells us that the Holy Spirit's presence brings freedom (2 Corinthians 3:17), but it also brings order (1 Corinthians 14:33). Only an all-knowing God could offer both simultaneously, designed to meet the demands of each situation.

In the home, we have spaces that need more freedom. We also have areas that need more order. Most personalities lend themselves to one or the other, and we must discipline ourselves into either structure or flexibility. The Holy Spirit convicts us of which we need most, graciously empowering us to build a "life-giving home." Sally Clarkson puts it this way:

> What greater joy can there be than to create a holding place
> for all that is sacred in life: faith, love, God, purpose, beauty,

relationships, creativity, fun, the art of life, safety, shelter, feasting? To foster education in many realms of interests, a classroom of life where foundations of morality are taught and modeled and wisdom is learned. To build an environment that contains everything necessary for people of all generations—from babies to the elderly—to live healthy and well in community. . . . Creating a lifegiving home, then, is a long process taken one step, one season at a time.[4]

The spiritual disciplines of home take time. Home—not Rome!—wasn't built in a day, and that's an immense load off our shoulders. We need not change everything at once or shame ourselves for the places in need of growth. Grace, not shame, leads to true discipline, and godly discipline makes us more like Jesus.

In Richard Foster's famous book *Celebration of Discipline*, twelve spiritual disciplines are outlined, structured into three groups of inward, outward, and corporate discipline types. These are by no means exhaustive, but they do sum up the habits of spiritual formation most often described in the Bible.[5]

Inward Disciplines:

- Meditation: the practice of meditating on the truth of God's Word
- Prayer: communing with God spirit to Spirit
- Fasting: periodically abstaining from food to become more spiritually aware and connected
- Study: the discipline of regular time in God's Word

Outward Disciplines:

- Simplicity: using money for purposes outside your own needs; owning only what you need

- Solitude: spending undistracted time alone with God
- Submission: deferring to others out of love for Christ; rejecting pride
- Service: giving time to others; sacrificing time like one would money, trusting God to provide

Corporate Disciplines:

- Confession: confessing sins to fellow believers for comfort and prayer
- Worship: worshiping God together through music, the Word, and sacraments
- Guidance: encouraging and advising one another in the life of Christ
- Celebration: practicing gratitude in community

The first four most often take place in our personal quiet time with God. Many Christians see them as relegated to an hour in the morning (or less, or not at all). We are taught to segment our time into neat, productive blocks; the inward disciplines belong in the "quiet time" block. Like I learned after I had my first baby, such spiritual disciplines must be flexible and lived throughout the day, even as we discipline ourselves to meet God at a specific time in the morning or evening. Yes, quiet times are important, but God is not trapped within them. He is with us every day, all day, in every task!

The outer disciplines are harder to contain. They require as much or more commitment, and they also require more intention in community. For instance, owning only what you need affects every waking hour, not just the quiet-time moment. We must decide—in the Starbucks drive-through—if the discipline of simplicity is a choice we are willing to make. Submission, too, escapes the time block. We must reject pride all day long, choosing humility and sacrificing some of our desires to serve those God has entrusted to our care.

The corporate disciplines require even more commitment because they cannot be enacted apart from the presence of other Christians. Spiritual disciplines *cost something.* But like any good investment, they pay dividends that are far more precious than what was first laid down.

These twelve disciplines reveal themselves in the routines and tasks of home. You need not escape to a monastery to find intimacy with God. The to-do list doesn't need to come to a neat and tidy close for you to experience strong faith, deep intimacy, and security in the arms of our Father. It can happen right here, right now, on this floor, at this table, in this laundry room. Spiritual discipline is woven into the fabric of a spiritual home; we can meet God by mopping floors. Here are some practical ways these disciplines show themselves in our homelife and can be pursued in the midst of daily tasks.

BIBLE STUDY

I will always be an advocate for early morning study time. I've tried a variety of models over the years, changing the time, bending flexibly with the demands of work and small babies and weird schedules, but early morning is how I remain the most consistent. That said . . . Scripture is not a "one and done" deal. Scripture is meant to saturate us all day long. Though I do spend time throughout the day meditating, praying, and memorizing Scripture, I also spend thirty to forty minutes studying Scripture in the morning at least three times a week. Nothing can replace what I learn from reading words on a page, prioritizing the study of Scripture so my soul can go deep into God's love.

During this time I read an assigned passage for the day, pull out the primary principle, and pray about that principle for a bit. I like to rewrite passages in my own words, often as prayers back to God. Then I'll pick a verse to meditate on throughout the day. Do I forget what I studied sometimes? Sure! But over the years I've read through the Bible so many times, the layers of repetition have laid a foundation in my soul. Every time I study I add a little more to the character God is building in me. I may not feel like anything is changing, but it is. God is creating a depth and strength by sheer exposure to His heart that will show up later in my life right when I need it.

MEDITATION

The Scriptures we pull out from our time in the Word can be turned around in our minds and memorized on our lips. I'll confess: I'm terrible at memorization. But Glenna Marshall made this persuasive case for memorization: "We already have all the love and approval we could ever need from God in Christ. We pray, read our Bibles, fellowship with the church, share the gospel, fast, give, serve, and yes—memorize Scripture—because we are *already* loved by God. Our spiritual disciplines help us to grow in awareness of that love."[6]

So as you go about your daily tasks, speak the Word of God out loud. As you wipe counters: "Fear not, for I am with you; be not dismayed, for I am your God" (Isaiah 41:10). As you fold laundry: "He who dwells in the shelter of the Most High will abide in the shadow of the Almighty" (Psalm 91:1). As you pack your bag for work: "Commit your work to the LORD, and your plans will be established" (Proverbs 16:3). The truths of Scripture teach me who God is, and as I dwell on who He is, I more fully understand myself. In days gone by, most people didn't own a Bible. They memorized Scripture as it was transmitted orally. Memorizing what we study and writing it in visible places around the house internalizes God's truth. I write verses on my bathoom mirrors and on the window I look through while I wash dishes. I tack three-by-five index cards above my desk, carry them in my purse, and set them by the stove:

"Surely, LORD, *you bless the righteous; you surround them with your favor as with a shield" (Psalm 5:12 NIV).* The truths simmer in my soul; I whisper them under my breath. I don't have to leave the pot I'm stirring to meet God. His sanctuary is here.

PRAYER

Meditation naturally lends itself to prayer, just as Bible study lends itself to meditation. The three do go together, but they don't have to be restricted to quiet time! Prayer is the gift of constant communication with the Lover of our souls. We can pray all day, in any circumstance. The worries and anxieties I like to mull on as I mindlessly vacuum or prep lunches for homeschool co-op turn into requests and questions: *I feel unseen. I don't know what to do. Your Word gives light; will You give me light here?* Sometimes I assign certain prayer topics to specific tasks: pray for the children when you do dishes three times a day; pray for the city when you feed the farm animals; pray for your husband with each laundry item folded. A physical action leading to intimacy with God: *a liturgy.*

Fasting, submission, solitude, simplicity, service—each discipline can be fitted to your homelife and tasks. If you're fasting lunch for the day but preparing it for an elderly parent, you're invited to pray more ardently in the Spirit as your hunger pangs are felt. Perhaps you're rejecting pride every time you bend to scrub toilets, choosing submission and service as you do. Maybe the rigid boredom of pulling weeds is the solitude your soul needs to come close to the Savior.

The home facilitates spiritual discipline like nowhere else. Here there is no one checking up on our progress. There is no corporate checklist to meet. The very thing we resent—the lack of measurable growth—is the means of our freedom. It is the means of relationship and spiritual depth.

Of course, cultivating the spiritual disciplines at home will sometimes require cutting back. Spiritual discipline has a cost. The disciplines point us to areas of compromise: ways we've allowed sin to creep into our homes; things that are stealing, killing, and destroying the joy God offers. The disciplines of deep spirituality remind me to fix my mind on what is good, pure, and noble. They draw my attention to media I should remove from my daily routine or words I shouldn't share with others, anger I need to submit to God's Spirit and resentment I need to release. The disciplines we pursue invite us to ask honest questions about the homelife we're creating. Here are some questions to ask as you practice these disciplines:

Meditation: *What about my homelife stops my joy in God and others? Is this under my control? What has God empowered me to change?*

Silence: *Is my home ever silent or still? Is it a constant stream of media, radio, sports, and phone use? How can I facilitate and accept silence (aside from human noise) here?*

Fasting: *What is God asking me to cut out or cut back? Where have I given in to excess? What is distracting me from God's purpose in this home?*

Celebration: *Do I make community a priority? Is my home a place where people can feel safe and loved? What have I allowed to keep me from obedience in hospitality?*

As we ask these questions, God grants us the grace to change. He shows us where we need more flexibility—opening our schedule to have time to host—or where we need more order (creating chore lists, putting a cleaning routine in place, or doing a load of laundry a day). Wherever we are at in our journey, God's grace empowers us through our mistakes and failings to build rhythms of purposeful life.

ROUTINES: RHYTHMS OF LIFE ON PURPOSE

After I learned how much routine could lead to freedom, I began to like routines for the sake of routines. But when our family went through a season of severe financial insecurity, coupled with my autoimmune diseases, three young children, and a young business, my routines began to slide. The negative voices of people from my past added to the burden: people who told me I was rigid, too structured, and not spontaneous enough. I spent almost two years being more flexible than ever before; I still had routines for the basics, but I didn't get up as early, I skipped days in my cleaning and laundry systems, and didn't stay on track with the things I knew would help the house run smoothly. God was gracious for that season, but I also received clear confirmation: my routines were not in the way of spontaneity, joy, or freedom . . . they facilitated it.

My season with reduced routines actually led to *more* stress, not less. I was paralyzed by decisions. I took forever to figure out what task to do next, procrastinated endlessly, and often called it "giving myself grace." But it didn't look like grace when, on Saturday, I had a mountain of laundry to fold! My break from routines may have been a season, but it's not a season I'll return to. I've learned that truly life-giving routines remove stress during stressful seasons. I would have been better off ignoring the negative voices and doing what I knew would help me thrive.

Perhaps you, too, have heard routines described as "inhibiting," "rigid," or "unbending." I think some people do plan their lives that way, but that's not a routine—that's a schedule. A routine is a simple order of events or tasks that eventually becomes habit. These habits remove decision fatigue, allowing our busy brains to take care of tasks without conscious effort (who would like less effort?! Me!). They are rhythms of life, purposefully chosen so that we may be energized and restored by the tasks we do each day.

The routines themselves are not "more spiritual." They facilitate the joy God offers—a joy we could experience every single day, if we weren't so overwhelmed by material things. Our culture does not facilitate joy; it facilitates passing happiness, often at the expense of long-term satisfaction. Surrounded by things, we find ourselves exhausted managing them. Routines free us to follow God's heart for our specific home and life stage: whether that's an apartment or your first house or your fifth move in six years.

Routines are habits in structured form. As stated previously, they remove excess decision-making (and therefore excess stress). I have home routines for:

- laundry
- dishes
- cleaning
- homeschooling
- yard and farm tasks
- any area that tends to get forgotten, stress me out, or demand weekly time

Some things are one-off tasks you can't plan for, but when the majority of repetitive home tasks are integrated into a routine, they become a natural part of life—automatic. Good routines lead to an almost-accidental rhythm of peace, innately felt and experienced because of intentional work up front.

CASTING A VISION FOR YOUR DAILY TASKS

Before we can create routines for the home, we have to start with vision. I define *vision* as a clear set of values or intentions for the future. These values are the foundation for goals, tasks, and priorities. No two homes will have the same exact strategy. And out of that vision, priorities will flow. Naomi's priorities as a single working woman were different from mine as a young mom of two. Aside from God, family, and community, how she tended her home and where her tasks fell in importance differed from mine. Yours, too, will differ because your life is unique and special. You have your own work, family, friends, community, and city. The tasks you do reflect that uniqueness. Your vision must be customized to where God has you, and out of this your priorities will flow.

Vision-Casting Questions:

- What are my core values? (Name three to five.)
- What do I love about my current homelife, routines, and tasks?
- What creates the most stress?
- How am I affected by these stressful habits/tasks?
- When I think about my current home habits, why do I do what I do?
- If those tasks no longer stressed me (were completed regularly), how would I feel?
- What do I want my homelife to be like in one year?
- What do I want to see more of in my home? Less of?
- What is the first change I could make?

Comb through your answers and compile a one-paragraph vision statement for the homelife you long for. Here's an example:

In one year I want my home to feel less cluttered and easier to maintain. I want to enjoy my kids more and not just pick up messes. This aligns with my core values of hospitality, peace, and joyful connection. Dealing with toys stresses me out the most, so I will concentrate on decluttering so I can spend more time with family and friends.

When you've answered these questions, you'll be on your way to a clearer understanding of what needs to change in your routines.

You'll be able to narrow in on the areas in need of more discipline or flexibility. You may even be able to discern what spiritual practices can be integrated into certain tasks! With your vision clarified, you can now determine priorities. If you envision a home that is hosting-ready, but you constantly feel stressed by cleaning, your priority for the next year should be on cleaning routines or decluttering. Yes, laundry still matters, but it can wait. It's not as great a stressor and it's not moving you toward your vision, so it's not as high a priority right now. Concentrate on creating routines for the places you want to see change first.

Based on the example vision statement, the home priorities might be:

- decluttering and donating toys
- organizing toys into bins
- creating a process for screening gifts as they come into the house
- implementing a cleaning routine with a different zone each weekday

These priorities determine what I would say yes or no to: I might decline a bin of boys' clothes because it's more clutter for me to manage. I might say yes to a half hour of cleaning each morning rather than binge cleaning on weekends. Vision → priorities → routines.

NOT ANOTHER TO-DO LIST

I developed my routines over several years, adjusting and changing them with each life stage. The process I used to create routines was not locked in to new motherhood or when I worked full time at an office. It was and is customizable for any life stage. Grab a notebook or use the margins for the following section, because we're going to develop a routine right now.

1. **Write down everything that stresses you out during the day.** Some people call these "pain points." What makes you anxious, upset, or cranky when you get home (or your spouse walks in the door)? For me, these are:

   ☐ a messy house
   ☐ a sink full of dishes
   ☐ missing a workout
   ☐ trying to make a meal while a child is whining
   ☐ staying up too late
   ☐ getting up after my kids are already awake

   Stress makes things feel like they're out of control, but look at the list above—all of those things are *under my control*! I want my daily routine to reduce stress, not increase it. But before we deal with solutions to those problems, we must make a separate list of "time suckers."

2. **Write down the things in your day that take extra time.** For example, things you do, even habits you didn't know you had, that whittle away five minutes here and there. My list included:

   ☐ picking out an outfit for myself
   ☐ scrolling through social media
   ☐ rechecking email
   ☐ doing *all* the dishes at the end of the day, when I want to go to bed
   ☐ jumping from one chore to another impulsively

Each of these things uses up precious time in tiny increments. They seem harmless in the moment, but when you
look back on the day, wondering why you didn't have time to
work, pursue passions, or spend time with your kids—*these*
are the culprits.

3. **Now combine these two lists. Is there anything on the
   second list that might be contributing to the first?** For
   instance, my social media scrolling is probably why I was
   up too late. Staying up too late is probably why I was
   getting up when my kids do. There's a domino effect
   from lacking discipline that's actually *in the way* of my joy
   at home. These sneaky bad habits are actually stressing
   us out. They might seem harmless, but they are hurting
   us. We can help ourselves out by bringing ourselves
   under control by the Spirit's strength, disciplining those
   tendencies, and freeing ourselves to enjoy our lives more.

4. **Now that you have your list, ask yourself: What can I do
   to solve these problems?** Take a moment to brainstorm
   ideas. No such thing as a bad idea! Think of a few things
   you could change or implement that would help alleviate
   those stressors in your life. For my previous example, this
   might be:

   ☐ Turn phone off at 9:00 p.m.
   ☐ Buy a real alarm clock so I'm not tempted to scroll when
      using my phone to set an alarm.
   ☐ Get up thirty minutes before the kids.

5. **Create routines to relieve these problem areas.** Now that
   you know these, you can work on creating routines that
   remove decision-making, which exhausts your brain, and

allow you to make tasks a habit. This in turn will free
you to concentrate on more important things. Let's start
by reviewing your list of stressors and time sucks. Read it
again.

As you saw in my stressor and time-sucker lists, I was struggling
to find time to clean, do dishes, and make meals. Yet somehow
I found time to wander around my closet and check my friends'
Facebook feeds. To stop these distractions, I created systems for
the tasks while also implementing boundaries on my time sucks.
We will talk about those boundaries later. For now, let's talk about
the systems. I broke down the tasks over the course of my week.
Rather than try to do laundry when I feel like it or all in one day, I
designate certain types of laundry for certain days of the week (we
will talk more about this in the "Liturgy of Laundry" chapter):

Laundry:

- Monday—sheets and towels
- Tuesday—Josh's and my clothes
- Wednesday—kids' clothes
- Thursday—rags and farm towels
- Friday—specialty items

I do the same thing with my cleaning schedule, doing a deep
clean on one area of the house each day of the week, and picking
up all toys/messes each night before bed:

Cleaning:

- Monday—main floor
- Tuesday—bathrooms
- Wednesday—bedrooms

- Thursday—main floor (in my house, we clean the most used area twice a week)
- Friday—deep-clean areas as needed

Dishes:

I discipline myself to do the dishes (for the first years of our marriage, this was by hand—we had no dishwasher) after each meal. This way all I have in the evening are dinner dishes, which Josh helps with.

HOW IT WORKS

So if it were Monday, I'd be washing sheets and towels. I would also be cleaning the living room. By doing only doing a portion of the laundry a day, only cleaning one room in the house, and pre-planning/preparing meals, I would rarely fall behind on home management. By dedicating thirtyish minutes a day, it would be done. This allows me to be completely present with my family and really *enjoy* life, not just manage it.

Now it's your turn. Taking your list of stressors, think about how you can make a routine to relieve that stress. If you get home from work at five thirty, starving, but have to look through the pantry to figure out dinner and don't end up eating until six thirty, it's time to meal plan! Designate some meals for the week based on the ingredients in your pantry. Set the ingredients on the counter the night before so when you get home, you're ready to go.

If you're not staying on track with fitness, set a more reasonable goal (maybe three times a week instead of five). Choose what kind of workout you'll do, which days you'll probably do it (but be flexible), and choose two different times of day you can do the workout. This way, if one time doesn't work out, you have a backup. (When I was working full time, I would either do my workout at 5:00 a.m. or on my lunch break, which was an hour long.)

See how this works? By giving yourself flexible routines and optional times for tasks, you relieve stress without locking yourself into a rigid schedule—and you *still* get done what you want to accomplish. (This works with academics too. Sketch out your syllabus into your planner and choose a few days of the week to really focus on certain subjects. Maybe designate Tuesday after class for your English homework, for instance.)

1. **Create a weekly plan.** I'm steering away from the word *schedule* here. It is very important that you *not* hold yourself to an hourly schedule. If you make a daily routine based on rising at six thirty but you sleep through the alarm or your baby wakes up raring to go at six, your whole routine goes down the tubes. Instead, *abide by a rhythmic routine* following the same *order*, not the same *hours*.

Planning takes work on the front end but brings peace in the long run. Before I dropped the hourly schedule, I was stressing myself out by doing everything at once or impulsively doing chores as I saw them. *Weekly planning means you don't even have to decide about what you need to do: you just look at the plan.*

To make a weekly plan, look over your weekly commitments and write down whatever is regularly occurring. You can use a planner or Google Calendar; you just want it all in one place.

Some Tips:

- *Remember, it's a rhythm, not an hourly schedule.* If you have kids, go with the flow of your baby's current schedule. Don't fight your season.
- *Leave holes in your routine.* I have several times throughout the day when I can do laundry, in case something happens and I can't do it at the usual moment.

- *Don't ever be afraid to schedule in a nap or rest time when needed.*
- *Underwhelm yourself.* Don't ask too much, and set reasonable expectations. For instance: Don't start out your fitness journey planning to work out five times a week. Maybe start with two, then work up to three, and so on.
- *Planning is only stressful if you are adding work to your life.* Some people think planning stresses them out *more.* But this planning is intended to lighten your workload, making it more efficient so you have time for the things you love.
- *Remember the goal: to be less stressed, more joyful, fully content in your home, and more fulfilled in the life God has given!*

Once I've made my plan, each Sunday night I look at the week and write down:

- appointments and outside commitments first (calendar items, meetings, social dates);
- my laundry, cleaning, and meal plans (for some, this might be academic assignments);
- my three to five work tasks that *must* get done (if you're not working outside the home, you could choose three to five top home or family projects); and
- toddler activities and homeschool lessons.

Sunday, or whatever day is the start of your week, is the "big picture" day. You get a good idea of what the week's demands will be, when you'll be home the most and the least. As you look at your recurring appointments, think about your routines. Try to schedule the easiest routines for the busiest days. For example, on Tuesdays we host Bible study, so Tuesday is my lightest cleaning and laundry day; it's also the day I make the most Crock-Pot dinners.

EVENING ROUTINES

As part of my evening routine, I lay several things out for the next morning: my Bible, my journal, and my planner (open to the next day). On each day of my planner I have written:

- my workout plan (Pilates or walking three miles);
- the cleaning assignment (living room, kitchen, etc.);
- my allotted Bible reading (I'm reading chronologically through the Word);
- breakfast, lunch, and dinner ideas and plans (Josh cooks dinner, but I'm in charge of my own lunch); and
- the laundry for that day.

After our kids go to bed around eight o'clock, I enjoy some time reading or hanging out with Josh, then head to bed by ten to read or watch a show with Josh. I don't really *want* to go to bed early, but I know it's the best choice so I can start the day with plenty of margin. Your evening routine will look different from mine, but what matters is that you have one. I also like to set out coffee supplies, breakfast items, or anything I use in the morning to save time when I get up.

MORNING ROUTINES

Each night when I review the next day, I sketch out a customized morning routine based on the day ahead. For instance, my day will look different on Mondays because our kids have their homeschool group at nine. I won't do any cleaning before we leave the house. But on Tuesdays, by nine o'clock I would be cleaning, doing laundry, and laying out our homeschool work.

I use an index card to write out the *order* in which things should happen the following morning. But importantly, *there are no hourly slots*! Even if I wake up a half hour late, I can still follow the order and get most things done.

Next Steps:

- Schedule time on Sunday night to plan your week ahead, writing down outside assignments, class work, and meetings first.
- Take the routines you made and plug them into your weekly plan.
- Think of a simple morning and evening routine that works for your lifestyle.

MAKE GOOD TO-DO LISTS

Your weekly plan is, in a way, a list. It's a list spread out over a span of time. But you also need a more specific list for each day, which is where my morning routine comes into play. Here are some quick tips for making good lists that actually get checked off:

- *Pick a* kind *of list that works for you.* I like to write my list by hand because that action helps my brain relax. I also have firm boundaries for my phone use, and I don't want to be picking up my phone all day to check off a list. I want to be able to put my phone away and still know what needs to get done. Find a type of list—handwritten or digital—that works for you *and* allows you to still keep healthy boundaries with your phone (if every time you're checking your list you're also on Instagram, digital is probably not a good option for you, productivity-wise).
- *Keep lists of bigger projects distinct from daily lists.* I keep my monthly, weekly, and daily goals on the fridge, where I can be reminded of my priorities at a glance. Then I can break those down into smaller tasks for my daily list.
- *Start with the easy items.* I like to check off "fold laundry" and "vacuum living room" because they are simple and quick tasks that help me feel like I'm gaining momentum.

- *Break down the big tasks.* Instead of "paint the upstairs," write, "pick up paint from Lowe's, paint stairwell, move furniture to spare room, paint ceiling," and so on.
- *Make tasks specific.* This is *so important.* "Write research paper" is vague. Break it down: "write outline," "pick up library books for bibliography," and so on.
- *Set a timer.* For each task on the list, set a timer. (Or you can use the Pomodoro method: set a timer for twenty-five minutes for focused work, followed by a two- to five-minute break; do this five times and you'll be shocked by how much you get done.)[7]

THE TA-DA LIST

A "ta-da" list is a list of things you got done that may not have been on your to-do list. It's evidence of how much you actually did, even if not everything on your to-do list got checked off. I *love* this concept, and it's a great way to encourage yourself after a long day.

Next Steps:

- Look at your to-do list for today. Are your tasks specific? Do you need to break them down more?
- Put the most important tasks first and set a timer for doing them.
- Create a ta-da list to encourage yourself.

Charlotte Mason—who I mentioned earlier—taught that parents and teachers were responsible to teach habits and routines to children so they could build upon those habits as they grew. "It rests with parents and teachers to lay down lines of habit on which the life of the child may run henceforth with little jolting or miscarriage, and may advance in the right direction with the minimum of effort."[8] If your parent or teacher did not lay down the rails of habit, it's not too late. It will take more effort, but you can still "advance in the right direction." What Charlotte didn't say here is that such habits and routines don't just bless your children, if you have them; they also bless you! You walk away better equipped to steward what you're given. You walk away more content with what you have. You walk away less anxious, more in control, more grateful, more aware, and more able to serve others.

Your vision and priorities lead to routines, and routines lead to daily habits, and daily habits, over time, lead to the homelife you've always dreamed of: a life of purpose and peace.

IMPLEMENTING THE SPIRITUAL DISCIPLINE OF HOME

Armed with vision and ready with a routine, you might wonder: *What's next? How do I actually implement a purposeful routine?* For now, the best implementation of what you're learning is the *integration* of your spiritual life into your dirty-hands, dish-scrubbing, lunch-packing life. It's learning that these daily tasks are not in the way but are *the* way to truly knowing God's love, brought down in humble form to the "manger" of mundane. When I'm sorting the pile of shoes in our midwestern mudroom, there's nothing much glamorous here. But I can meet God in the sanctuary of a tile floor, speaking His truth with as much reverence as in the cathedral hall; and I can pour milk into a baby's proffered cup with as sacred an intention as the priest raising the Eucharist. I can pray as fervently on my knees, wiping maple floors with a ragged cloth, as I can at the front of a church at altar call.

Yesterday the children went for a walk with me. The leaves were all gone, brown and frozen beneath our boots. We walked briskly to avoid the wind. "Look!" they shouted. "The trees are hugging!" I looked, and there the beech tree grew crooked, bent sideways a bit as it wrapped itself around a birch. They embraced in a lovely dance, unnoticed by all except the smallest of us.

The routines of home and the spiritual disciplines of faith embrace like these beech and birch trees. They wrap around each other and support one another, often unnoticed—until we're on our knees, tending to things in a posture of prayer.

THE LITURGY OF HOMEMAKING

Emmanuel:
  You who made a home with us—so imperfect and undeserving:
  help us make a home for others; a home built on You.
  You are the cornerstone of our foundation,
  the rock immovable.
  The Word became flesh and dwelt among us,
  You dwell among us still by Your Spirit.
  May Your goodness permeate our homes.
  May we discipline ourselves to seek You.
  And as we scrub, wash, tend, mend, and create beauty here
  may it be an echo of Your Creator heart,
  an invitation, a garden glimpse,
  of eternity on earth.
Amen

CHAPTER 8

Salt of the Earth

The Liturgy of Cooking

THE TABLES I'VE JOINED HAVE VARIED IN SIZE—THE
cooking styles and skills varied as well—but in each one I was
blessed by the thought and effort. Grandma's roast beef, tender
and saltless, blessed in a different way than Mom's delicious pear-
glazed ham and mashed potatoes. Then there is the zuppa Toscana
our friend Joel makes, the apple crisp Hali brings, or the amazing
chalupas Josh cooks from scratch, made after grinding the grain
himself. *Delight.*

My daughter learned to make scrambled eggs and for a while
would block off the upstairs hallways so she could put finishing
touches on her work. She'd carry the tiny white plate to our bedroom door and come tiptoeing in, giant hopeful eyes peering at us
with joy. Scrambled eggs are simple. But love is deep. It's not the
food but the heart behind it that blesses most.

Before I had kids, when I was still working outside the home,
cooking was the bane of my existence. Perhaps I should rephrase:
cooking on *weekdays* was the bane of my existence. I didn't mind it

on weekends, when I had plenty of time to be creative and nothing had to fit into a Tupperware to be reassembled later. Packing *the God-forsaken lunches* made my life miserable. I didn't want to eat grilled chicken, rice, and broccoli every day of the week. But I also didn't want to prepare five different lunches. Then I had to think about dinner for one person and make something I wouldn't have to eat for ten days based on giant portion sizes. Tasks like these made cooking a dread rather than a joy.

I didn't completely figure this out as a single person, so I faced it again when I had toddlers. Toddlers also don't eat large portions, are easier to feed if you prep ahead, and probably shouldn't eat the same thing every day if you want them to get adequate nutrition . . . so I found myself in the same situation as before. Dread and food became simultaneous, especially around 4:30 p.m.

But I didn't want to dread the dinner hour. I didn't want to miss out on 365 hours of the year because I couldn't find a way to enjoy them. Hours pile up into days, which pile into years; years of resenting time God has given. I knew in my soul this was not how God wanted me to live a significant portion of my life. I began creating a system for meal planning, shopping, and cooking that allowed me to be creative. I could make what I liked, or what I had time for, with all the ingredients on hand. The freedom brought back my joy!

Then . . . our season changed again. Around our ninth year of marriage, I started working afternoons (rather than mornings) through the dinner hour. Josh didn't really know how to cook, had never meal planned, and rarely grocery shopped. (I'd started enjoying my systems so much, I didn't let him!) I was shocked to discover just how good he was (and is) at managing our meal routine once he had the chance. Now he cooks on weekdays; I assist with lunches and weekend dinners. Through all seasons, I've learned to see cooking as a way to worship, as a liturgy—a physical act directing attention to God—in the midst of daily life at home.

WHAT SCRIPTURE SAYS ABOUT FOOD

Scripture speaks about food extensively. Food is often used as a symbol, perhaps most obviously in the act of Communion (or Eucharist) where bread and wine represent the body and blood of Christ. Scripture speaks about our relationship with food as well as the important role it plays in being human:

- "Go, eat your bread with joy, and drink your wine with a merry heart, for God has already approved what you do" (Ecclesiastes 9:7).
- "Better is a dinner of herbs where love is than a fattened ox and hatred with it" (Proverbs 15:17).
- "And wine to gladden the heart of man, oil to make his face shine and bread to strengthen man's heart" (Psalm 104:15).
- "So, whether you eat or drink, or whatever you do, do all to the glory of God" (1 Corinthians 10:31).
- "He who supplies seed to the sower and bread for food will supply and multiply your seed for sowing and increase the harvest of your righteousness" (2 Corinthians 9:10).
- "He who gives food to all flesh, for his steadfast love endures forever" (Psalm 136:25).

In the Old Testament, food is associated with hospitality, celebration, and even worship (such as the bread of the Presence in the tabernacle and temple in Exodus 25:30). Whether you were a nomadic Middle Eastern people living in tents or a medieval European in a wooden house or an American Puritan on the New England coast, cooking food was a necessary daily task. At some point you would be harvesting it, preparing it, eating it, storing it, and saving it. Not much has changed.

Food marks my most formative memories. The pot roast my mom put in the oven early on Sunday morning, ready to eat when we got home from church; the delicious chocolate chip bars my sister would make for teenage hangouts; the incredible salads my aunt brought to family gatherings. There was the wedding of our college friends, where cake was replaced with eighteen different kinds of pie, set on tiered stands around the reception hall. Or the smell of decaf coffee and s'mores around the patio fire as Josh and I sit with our friends till much too late at night, the children falling asleep to a movie inside. Food marks my memories like a sign, a marker of my experiences, scents and tastes reminding me of the company I kept.

There have been cooking disasters, like the time I attempted ladyfinger cookies and had none of the ingredients, so I substituted everything in the recipe (surprise: it didn't work). My short stint in sourdough sent me running back to yeast bread. (I can't feed things that are supposed to feed *me*.) But there were also magnificent meals, cascading charcuterie boards, and dinner parties showcasing the skill of our friends. Some meals are small, like the sushi Josh and I learned to make for at-home date nights. Others are large, like the chili I cooked for all seventy attendees of our annual harvest party (for that one, I had to cook the soup in a deep fryer used for Thanksgiving turkeys—the only pot big enough—standing on a stool to stir it with two spoons taped together so I could reach the bottom!).

Notice that all my memories of food are also connected to people. Food is a central element for gatherings, something to connect over, talk about, and delight in. While idolatry of food should be avoided, celebration and food go hand in hand—even in the Bible, as I mentioned before. The Passover meal in particular uses food to symbolize the deliverance of God (Exodus 12). Food must be eaten for survival, but food is not *just* about survival. The ways we cook and present it have the power to build community and love.

When I'm cooking freezer meals for the next two weeks or making peanut butter sandwiches for our homeschool co-op lunch boxes, I tend to forget the power of food. In that moment, cooking annoys. The daily task of cooking can feel burdensome and dreary. Perhaps you, like me, dread the Tupperware packing or the five o'clock evening hour. In this chapter I hope to lift our eyes beyond the pots and stovetops to the underlying spiritual *purpose* in this daily act, and the opportunity for worship within it. Then I'll give some practical tips for managing meals and making this part of your home culture a blessing rather than a curse.

GIVING THE GIFT OF FOOD

I've told you about my grandma and her penchant for unsalted beef. Salt or not, Grandma made a mean roast, and it was always accompanied by mashed potatoes, green bean casserole, rolls, and banana bread. Grandma's way of loving us was through food. I've found food to be a wonderful mediator to such a love—and to deep spiritual conversations.

Over the years food has acted as the go-between to connect across a table. As we pass a salad or a loaf of bread, we get to know a person's soul. Over coffee or tea we can open our hearts, hear stories, and learn things we never knew. Food facilitates joy and connection; the table is a place to fill a plate and fill a heart. Food is the gift we give, leading to the ultimate gift we give: a welcoming presence and a safe place to land. The act of leading people toward Christ with truth and grace is called "discipleship," which means when Christians eat together they are, in a sense, discipling people over food.

Discipleship around the table is not as formal as it sounds. Perhaps you picture a sermon-style lecture or a carefully programmed testimony time. No, discipleship is simply walking hand in hand with people toward God, and there are few places as suited for that as a dinner table (or brunch, lunch, or coffee table).

This is especially true for children, who are always hungry and eager for a snack. In fact, mealtime discipleship became so popular with our kids, it became a regular occurrence—sometimes three times a day.

This discipleship routine worked because food was the center. Three times a day we need to eat; three times a day we sit down together. By taking that opportunity to ask good questions, read Scripture, and talk briefly about what God is doing, spiritual conversations become the rhythm of home. And it doesn't end with kids; spiritual discipleship happens at tables in the most surprising and gentle of ways.

Like the time we heard an acquaintance's testimony of leaving atheism for Christ.

Or the time an unbelieving friend confessed their current spiritual thoughts.

Or when our child prayed confidently for the first time.

Or when we grieved a recent divorce, learned what it was like to leave extreme legalism, held the story of six consecutive miscarriages, or shared our own marriage struggles (and successes) with another couple at dinner.

All of it happened over food and, I believe, *because* of food. Food brings us together. The invitation says "dinner" but it implies "come and be known."

You might be wondering what this looks like practically. Mealtime discipleship for our children is much more specific than hosting a dinner; the intentions and audience are very different. With our children, we are actively teaching them scriptural truths. When hosting guests, that's not our goal. So when we sit down with our kids at a meal, we offer them a feast of food and a "feast" of learning. Card sets with prayer ideas are scattered on the table. A children's Bible is propped in the center. A booklet of easy theology questions for kids is available for the taking. There's "prayer topic dice" they can roll to decide what to pray about next, a stack of flashcards on the attributes of God, and memory verses we're working on. The children can choose whatever item strikes their fancy; we read it and discuss.

This approach to mealtime discipleship grounds us in a routine of worship (another liturgy!) while offering the children some autonomy in the process. They learn about God in short, natural tidbits; no lectures or long sermons from mom and dad. And this conversation continues beyond the meal. While we sit and eat, we "eat" from the Word of God, learning the patterns and stories of Scripture in ways we will not soon forget.

When adults come to dinner, mealtime discipleship looks different. We don't break out the prayer cards (though we do still pray over the meal!). Discipleship in this context is far less formal because friends and acquaintances are not children and have not consented to being taught at their evening meal. But discipleship is not just formal teaching; it is the life-on-life relationship pointing people to the love of God. Families, and single people, in homes are a force of stability and blessing to those living an anchorless life (or those simply seeking community). We don't have to preach to disciple. We can live our faith visibly, purely, and lovingly alongside them:

- Ask good questions. Small talk is essential when you're first getting to know one another, but you can take it deeper by asking a more vulnerable question: "Switching careers sounds challenging. What were you feeling during that transition?"
- Learn about their faith journey. What is their church background? What is their experience of faith?
- Don't pressure or push; listen.
- Be a light representing peaceful faith in God: no evangelistic urgency, no pressure to perform, no striving. You are simply enjoying God and inviting people to enjoy His blessings through your table.

What better place to disciple than over bread and cheese? A charcuterie board opens doors to conversation like few ministry activities I know.

PLANNING YOUR MEALS

However, meals, vital as they are, can be a stress point. When I was the primary cook in our early years of marriage, I hated having to figure out dinner at four in the afternoon. I also didn't like being forced into a rigid meal plan, because I love the creativity of cooking (I'm no gourmet chef, but I enjoy learning). To fix this, I planned meals on Sundays, choosing four to five different dinners for which I'd bought the ingredients, and I allowed myself to move them around during the week based on how I felt or what I was craving. I knew I wanted to eat foods that energized me; I didn't want to be dependent on caffeine. Due to the autoimmune disease I had for five years, I had to be diligent to eat protein at every meal, drink enough water, and avoid excess sugar. To be this intentional I had to plan my meals—another one of those added tasks to resent!

Though it's been hard at times, the routine of meal planning at the beginning of the week has helped me immensely with my health over the years and has even helped keep us to a healthy budget. We went through many ideations of meal planning, changing with the seasons: creative thirty-minute dinners, freezer meals, sheet pan roasts. I planned Crock-Pot meals for days we were busy or were having company over, just to relieve stress. Here is a quick list of how I handled meals in a busy season of small kids:

- In our early years, I planned all dinners two weeks at a time. Now Josh does our weekly meal planning and weekday cooking, and I cook on weekends. He focuses on dinners, making big enough recipes to eat leftovers the next day. Breakfasts are usually the same each morning and lunches may be leftovers or something easy to batch.

- If having company, choose meals you know by heart and ones that are simple to make. Tried-and-true recipes can be more easily doubled to feed a crowd (and don't be afraid to ask your guests to bring a side or dessert).
- To decrease my stress at mealtime, I try to keep a basket of easy lunch items for my kids. When my husband worked outside the home, I helped him pack his lunch the night before. (We made our lunches together when we were both working, and I occasionally made breakfasts for the week.) Some of my favorite breakfasts include:

    ☐ overnight oats—put in a container and leave till morning
    ☐ overnight chia pudding
    ☐ eggs and sourdough toast
    ☐ eggs and half an avocado
    ☐ baked oatmeal
    ☐ plain yogurt and honey or jam

Make a plan for whatever meal is the hardest, or wherever you tend to eat out the most. And remember: you're not doing this just for the sake of doing it. This is an act of stewardship, seen and loved by God.

There are countless ways to meal plan—even services you can hire to do it for you!—so this section is by no means exhaustive. It's just a starting place for you to customize and adapt for your season.

PLANNING FOR ONE PERSON

One of the biggest challenges of cooking for one person is ingredients: they are sold in larger quantities than one person needs! Most recipes cook batches for families, and who wants to eat chili every day for a week? (Some of you do, and no shame if that's the case!)

Saturday night may be a better planning day than Sunday for those who are working outside the home. If you plan your meals on Saturday, you can schedule a pick-up grocery order for Sunday after church, or do a delivery by Sunday evening—in time to have everything you need for packing lunch! A few other tips for making one-person meals a liturgy, which is, as a reminder, a physical action pointing to God's provision:

- Check your pantry and fridge before making your grocery list. What needs to be used up? Choose two to three ingredients and find recipes using these, then add the remainder to your order.
- Invest in some glass Tupperware (you can thrift this, then wash it) and freeze leftovers if you don't want to eat them right away. You'll have dinner ready for busy days.
- Choose meals you actually love, not the meals you think you *should* be eating. What brings you joy? What makes you excited, or at least a little less dread-filled? Choose those recipes.
- Add snacks, not just lunches or dinners, to your meal rotation. For instance, make a batch of muffins each weekend for easy breakfasts or midday snacks on the go.
- Cook a large batch of meat (e.g., ground beef or shredded chicken) and use it multiple ways over the week.
- Be flexible! It's okay if you go off the plan. If you go out to dinner one night, bump your meal plan forward and make the next thing on the plan, or skip the day and stick with the original recipe.

PLANNING FOR COUPLES AND FAMILIES

When meal planning for two or more people, a few more factors are at play. We must consider preferences other than our own—find out what people like and don't like, and plan accordingly. As with cooking for one person, checking the pantry and fridge eliminates buying extra food or missing an ingredient you didn't know you needed. Setting aside a planning day (Saturday or Sunday) is also helpful.

In family settings, cooking is made more difficult by the rambunctious "witching hours" of 4:00–6:00 p.m., when children get energetic and busy *just* as you're putting dinner on the stove. A few tips for making this a time of celebration rather than an hour of sheer chaos:

- Turn it into a dance party. Let each child pick a playlist, rotating through their preferences over the week. We've done Disney classics, electronic beats, '90s country, and worship music. They dance and the parent cooks (joining in the dance too, of course!).
- Make 4:00–6:00 p.m. a special time when certain toys are brought out, to be put away when dinner is on the table.
- Incorporate the children. Give them responsibility. Let them help by setting the table, stirring the meat or pasta, filling water cups, lighting candles, or emptying the dishwasher. Playlists make a great accompaniment to chores too.

Meal planning for a family takes flexibility. Sports, activities, dinner invites—these interrupt the "plan" and can result in unused ingredients or extra spending. It's especially hard when you're accommodating the preferences and needs of family members after working all day. A few tips:

- Seek joy. Make meals you like, even if you do the same ones often. If it's easiest, schedule the same meals or types of meals on each weekday: pasta on Monday, beef dish Tuesday, Crock-Pot Wednesday, and so on.
- Eat the same thing for breakfast each day, or have a simple

list of options. Our kids started making their own breakfast at around two years old (with help) with simple meals like yogurt and granola, peanut butter toast, or berries and hard-boiled eggs.

- Keep easy snacks on hand: we have a drawerful of beef sticks, string cheese, baby carrots, and apples.
- Plan the easiest meals for the busiest days. For example, make smoothies for lunch.
- Use an Instant Pot or Crock-Pot liberally (these can be found at thrifts or on Facebook Marketplace).
- Try prepping ingredients the night before while listening to a podcast (this works for anyone, not just families). Pop them in a Tupperware, chopped and ready to go for dinnertime. Cook the meat ahead of time, and chop the other items for use later in the week.
- Are you an electronic or print recipe person? I like printed recipes, so I use cookbooks for planning. Whatever is most natural to you will help you plan.
- Communicate openly about your needs and desires. In our home, whoever isn't cooking does the dishes with the kids. (Some nights this doesn't occur because Josh has a church meeting or I'm headed out to meet friends, but it's a general rhythm for when we're all home working together.)
- After leftovers cool, pack them up for tomorrow's lunch.

Amy Gannett

My friend Amy is a church planter, the founder of Tiny Theologians (a theology ministry for kids), and a wife and mom to three—and she's also a master meal planner! Amy inspires me with her "feed the freezer" method of cooking. Each time she makes a meal, she doubles the recipe and freezes half for later. On busy weeks she can easily pull a meal out of the freezer for lunch or dinner. "I do it for my future self," she once told me, and I love that perspective! Amy's routine inspired me to try freezing recipes ahead so I could toss them into the Crock-Pot before soccer games. Future Phylicia always thanks me.

DIETARY NEEDS

When my chronic illness was at its peak, I went through multiple elimination diets to reduce inflammation. In these seasons our family abstained from gluten, sugar, eggs, dairy, and (it felt like) every other yummy thing under the sun to determine the underlying cause. We no longer have to do this, but it taught me how to cook and plan for strict dietary guidelines and to meal plan accordingly.

Here are a few tricks to help:

- Buy gluten-free flour in larger amounts from places like Costco, or grab cup-for-cup bags on sale and stock up. You can use this as a roux in soups, to make your own baked goods, or to have on hand if gluten-free guests come by.
- Keep flax and arrowroot in stock; flax can be used in a pinch to substitute for egg, and arrowroot for cornstarch.
- Almond milk can be a great substitute for dairy milk, but for those who can't have nuts, oat milk may be a better choice. Some can stomach goat milk much better than cow's, but it can be an acquired taste.
- Stock up on gluten-free frozen cookie dough for last-minute guests, or make it yourself.
- Kite Hill is a great-tasting dairy-free brand for cream cheese and other non-milk products that typically contain dairy.
- Plan paleo meals. These don't use dairy or grains, so you don't have to worry about substitutes.

THE SALT OF THE EARTH

In the Sermon on the Mount, Jesus told us His true followers will be recognized by how they "flavor" the world around them: "You are the salt of the earth. But if the salt loses its saltiness, how can it be made salty again? It is no longer good for anything, except to be thrown out and trampled underfoot" (Matthew 5:13 NIV). Salt adds flavor, but it's also a preservative. Grandma's roast beef came alive with a little salt; it brought out the richness and depth of her creation. And when storing food long-term, salt saves it from rot. In the same way, the way we steward the liturgy of cooking can help a community come alive with faith. Food can become a "saving grace," an arrow to the gospel, empowering people to look beyond the table to the God who loves their souls. Perhaps that sounds far-fetched to you right now, but I've seen it with my own eyes again and again. I've had the deep conversations over coffee and charcuterie; I've held the little hands as they prayed for the meal; I've seen tears cried and dried with a cloth napkin; I've heard the raw questions in candlelight—all because food was on the table and a simple task of meal-making was seen as God's work.

It seems so obscure, unseen, and repetitive. But the miracle of the Lord's Table in Communion points to an ongoing miracle at another table in community, where bread and wine still symbolize Jesus—and where His presence dwells just as much.

A Liturgy for Cooking

Lord God,
*   You who broke bread at a table*
*   and lifted the wine to represent Your blood:*
*   You created the substances which represent You.*
*   You sustain all things, even the things which sustain us.*
*   As I stir, boil, chop, and plate*
*   I see the eternal purpose of sustaining others*
*   from the abundance of Your provision.*
*   You have laid a table before us;*
*   our cups overflow with Your kindness.*
*   Goodness and mercy follow me:*
*   at breakfast, lunch, and dinner. My hands*
*   worship through the working, my prayers*
*   continue beyond the table.*
*   There are no leftovers with You.*
*   You have given us Your best, that we may share*
*   and serve and give again out of the abundance.*
*   O God, You are kind to include me in this mission*
*   of being salt to the earth.*
Amen

CHAPTER 9

A Beautiful Undoing

The Liturgy of Cleaning

EVERY DAY, WITHOUT FAIL, I WIPE COUNTERS. BY LUNCH-time those counters are covered with crumbs, so I wipe them again. At dinner, bedecked with spilled milk, apple juice, and cutting boards, I clear and wipe and reset . . . again. Then before bed, I do one more once-over, just to do it all again the next day.

Every day, without fail, I clean a floor. It might be the bedroom floor or the bathroom floor, the living room carpet or the heavily trafficked kitchen. I sweep or vacuum or mop, leaving what was once crumbly, clean.

Every day, without fail, the work I did earlier in the day descends slowly into dirt. It's like a funeral for my effort: "From dust to dust." If I look at cleaning as a meaningless repeated task, or if I idolize the result, my daily work to tend the home *could* feel aimless. But I believe these tasks have an aim: an intent, a focus, a plan. And when I look at my messed-up counters and the floor I just cleaned, I remember the aim.

Our liturgy of cleaning includes multiple practices and move-ments: sometimes we stand, sometimes we kneel, sometimes we bow, sometimes we walk. Each holy task of worship points to a God constantly "cleaning up" after His people. We are not alone in repetition. We are not alone in redoing the work. How many times a day does God pick up after His people? How many times a day does His grace catch me, hold me, restore me? Can I not bend to restore the places I've labored, in the same way He bends to restore His?

I think a theology of home is realized most in our view of cleaning. I'll talk about the spirituality of laundry, hospitality, and decoration too, but here in the liturgy of cleaning we find ourselves most susceptible to resentment. Here we face down the constant need to redo and restore. It can be discouraging, frustrating, exhausting. I suppose any ritual can adopt these traits when we lose the heart behind it, which is why we must center our hearts on the purpose of home tasks. We work to the glory of God! We worship through these daily tasks as fully as when we stand arms uplifted in our worship service at church.

I think about Jesus on the night before He died. There were so many pressing things to attend to, but instead Jesus knelt before His disciples and cleaned their feet. He washed away the dirt, sponging their caked ankles with a cloth. He moved through twenty-four sets of filthy toes, willing to get His holy hands dirty with the dust of the street. The work of cleaning was not too good for our Savior. But He didn't do this so the disciples could benefit once and forget: "When he had finished washing their feet, he put on his clothes and returned to his place. 'Do you understand what I have done for you?' he asked them. 'You call me "Teacher" and "Lord," and rightly so, for that is what I am. Now that I, your Lord and Teacher, have washed your feet, you also should wash one another's feet" (John 13:12–14 NIV).

This act of service, done through the task of cleaning, is a model for us to follow. We are expected to see such humble tasks as ways to emulate our Savior. Could cleaning our homes be a way to walk in His footsteps?

Cleaning and washing are acts of worship when done with a

worshipful heart. How do we move from seeing cleaning as worship to actually getting it done? Even if we recognize God's appreciation for our stewardship, working under the favor He abundantly supplies, we still have to actually *do* the work. And the work repeats itself. The key is routine.

Some of us are frustrated by cleaning because we have no good system to sustain it. Every time we clean, it becomes a domino effect of tasks and an hours-long endeavor leading to resentment and procrastination. This feeling of overwhelm need not be our reality! It is possible to live an extremely busy life and maintain a home that is tidy (note: I did *not* say "perfectly clean"). This tidiness is not a form of performative holiness but an act of stewardship of God's gifts. It equips us for hospitality (which we will talk about in a future chapter) and blesses us with less anxiety at home. In short, cleaning, when done well and without perfectionism, leads to more peace, more beauty, more rest, and more joy. And the key is to do *a little every day*; to make a habit of tending well.

A LITTLE EACH DAY

The habit-formation adage "what you do every day matters more than what you do once in a while" applies to the discipline of cleaning: cleaning a little every day is much easier than doing it all once a week. As a working mom, I understand the pull of children and commitments—I have many. But I also want to *enjoy* where I live, not be stressed out by it. So to bless myself and give my future self the gift of a beautiful, tidy environment, I do a little every day. If you have kids at home, they can and should be a part of this process; they can help too!

For ten years I've practiced what is called *zone cleaning*. When I lived in an apartment with two other college-aged women, we divided up the zones and assigned an individual to each. When first married and in our first apartment, I only had three zones: bathroom, living room, and kitchen. When we moved to a duplex with our new baby, I had four. And now I have five, with a repeat of the living room zone twice a week.

Zone cleaning works because it is manageable. Instead of using an entire weekend to clean, only to watch it progressively fall apart all week, you can do a little each day and some upkeep tasks every evening and morning. With these little repetitive tasks, the house doesn't descend into utter chaos. Here's how to do it.

First, you create zones. Divide your house into five areas (bathrooms, living room, kitchen, bedrooms, mud/laundry room); then number them in order of hardest to easiest to clean (1 being easy, 5 being hard). Each Sunday, you can schedule your zones this way: zones one and two on your busiest days, zones three, four, and five on your most flexible days.

Alternatively you can assign zones to a day of the week and never change them (this is what I do):

- Monday: main floor (living room and kitchen)
- Tuesday: bathrooms
- Wednesday: bedrooms
- Thursday: main floor again
- Friday: laundry room and/or deep-clean spots

These are the focused cleaning zones: the areas you'll vacuum, dust, wipe down, and rearrange as needed. However, for a fun little gift to yourself, try doing some tasks every day to keep up without much effort (quickly after meals, before leaving the house, or before bed):

- make your bed right after you get up; it finishes the room and creates a sense of immediate accomplishment
- load dishes and wipe counters after meals

- pick up toys and reset the pillows on couches after lunch and before bed (if at home)
- sort mail in the driveway and throw away junk before coming inside
- sweep floors
- wipe bathroom counters and clean shower drain

Each of these tasks takes no more than five to ten minutes, some as little as one minute. But by training yourself to clean as you go, you free yourself from the chaotic feeling of overwhelm at the end of the week.

PREPARING YOURSELF TO TIDY

If "a little each day" sounds annoying, hang in there. It might be an adjustment, but you're simply trading hours of work on a weekend for the same hours, broken up over the week. All time commitments are time *trades*; you're saying yes to one thing and no to another. If I say *yes* to cleaning all day on Saturday, I say *no* to going out for brunch with my friends or taking an impromptu hike with my kids. Sometimes skipping home tasks is the best choice; I'm not suggesting we put tasks ahead of people. But our home tasks also facilitate our relationships with people and therefore deserve our attention.

Some people (including myself) feel a low-level anxiety about everything hanging over them while they try to enjoy weekend activities. What if you could go into your weekend without that pressure? What if you had the entire weekend without home tasks, or with just a few, because you did a little every day during the week? It's worth a try!

But before we can make a solid cleaning routine, we must prepare ourselves to tidy. I'm no Marie Kondo, but I did have a Dutch grandma, and here's what I stock to be ready to clean in short increments during the week. I use nontoxic cleaners because my children are cleaning with me, but use whatever you prefer:

- Vacuum: I have a Shark with a hose attachment. A handheld might be nice as well.
- Spin mop: I use this occasionally on extremely dirty floors, like the mudroom.
- Cloth rags for dusting and mopping: You can use old pillows cases and t-shirts too.
- Cleaning scrub: Grandma used Borax; I make my own with baking soda.
- Toilet cleaner and scrubber: I use undiluted nontoxic cleaner, but if that grosses you out, a Clorox toilet cleaner is great too.
- Cleaning spray: For counters, dusting, showers, and more.
- Windex: For windows and mirrors.
- Rubber gloves: I wear gloves to protect my nails. *Priorities*.
- Dishwash detergent: This has multiple uses beyond dishes!
- Duster: For reaching cobwebs and corners.

These are stored in one location, ideally in a caddy or bucket for easy transportation. We keep our cleaning spray and a rag under the sink so the kids can wipe up spills on their own.

Before we talk about how to create your own custom cleaning routine, some of you might be wondering how to actually . . . clean the house. Maybe you were taught an all-or-nothing mentality, or maybe you didn't have a parent who knew how to care for the house. Here are a few tips for when you're going through your routine:

- **Grandma's mantra: look for dirt.** Keep your eyes open for things that need to be scrubbed, vacuumed, or wiped down. Look for water droplets on the front of the trash can, crumbs behind the KitchenAid mixer, and dirt behind the toilet. As you vacuum, wash, and sweep, look for dirt.

- **Use elbow grease.** You'll have to kneel, scrub, get in corners, and get a little dirty to make things clean. Don't be afraid to be thorough. When we leave those nasty little bits, they just get worse the next time.
- **Move things around.** When cleaning a counter, remove what's on it. Take everything off the stovetop to wipe it down. When cleaning a toilet, lift all the lids and wipe around them and behind them.
- **Move furniture.** If physically possible—no need to become Two Men and a Truck—move couches, chairs, and tables to vacuum behind them every other week. Use the vacuum hose to get underneath and inside the sofa as well.
- **Use a different cloth for windows, surfaces, and toilets.** Obviously, we don't want the toilet rag being used on the sink—gross! But the dusting rag can also shed cobwebs and fuzzies all over mirrors and windows. Use separate rags for each task, then wash them on hot with detergent and bleach.

With your cleaning items prepared, now you need a *plan*.

YOUR NEW TIDY PLAN

When cleaning a room, work from top to bottom:

- dust
- wipe
- sweep
- vacuum
- mop
- windows/mirrors (I do windows last in case any dust is thrown up from the vacuum.)

Here is the key: if you are doing this routine regularly (every week-ish) and a quick pickup each evening before bed, the gentle maintenance puts the brakes on overwhelm. Things might still pile up, mess up, and need a deep clean now and then, but not to the extreme of before. Time spent constantly cleaning, or whole weekends spent making up for the week, can be eradicated by breaking the tasks over a few days.

Following are two suggested cleaning schedules for different life stages to ease the struggle of constant upkeep. Remember: these are suggestions. No schedule will speak to every life. To figure out what works for you, ask yourself what days you want off each week. What days do you want a break from housework? Then break the zones over the remaining days. The following schedules give an idea of how long each task takes when done *thoroughly*, though not always perfectly (we're letting go of perfect).

WORKING FULL TIME OR IN SCHOOL:

- **Sunday: Look over your calendar and schedule zones** appropriate to busy days and flex days, or try the following task lists either early in the morning before work or right when you get home. As tempting as it is to retire as soon as you come through the door, if you keep the momentum for just twenty more minutes, you can wrap up your cleaning, eat dinner, and relax for the rest of the evening. Or you can get up twenty minutes earlier and have it done before heading in to work.

- **Monday: bathrooms**
  - ☐ Wipe down toilet (can use Lysol wipes in a pinch). (3 minutes)
  - ☐ Sweep floor. (3 minutes)
  - ☐ Dump trash into kitchen bin. (2 minutes)

- ☐ Wash sink and mirror. (5–7 minutes)
- ☐ Spray and scrub shower (can move this to deep-clean day if you're pinched for time). (10–15 minutes)
- ☐ Mop floor every two weeks. (30 minutes)

- **Tuesday: bedrooms**
  - ☐ Shake out curtains and dust curtain rod/walls. (5 minutes)
  - ☐ Vacuum floor; move nightstands and use hose to vacuum edges and under bed. (10 minutes)
  - ☐ Wipe down flat surfaces. (10 minutes)

- **Wednesday: living area**
  - ☐ Move items and dust flat surfaces. (10 minutes)
  - ☐ Vacuum floor, edges, under furniture, and between couch and chair cushions. (10 minutes)
  - ☐ Wash windows. (5–10 minutes)
  - ☐ Mop (really scrub) once a month if wood floor, more if you wear shoes in the house. (40–60 minutes)

- **Thursday: kitchen**
  - ☐ Dust surfaces and tops of cabinets. (10–15 minutes)
  - ☐ Wipe down sinks and counters. (5 minutes)
  - ☐ Wipe down front of fridge, dishwasher, and oven. (5 minutes)
  - ☐ Sweep or vacuum floor. (5 minutes)
  - ☐ Mop once a week. (30 minutes)
  - ☐ On grocery day, wipe out fridge shelves.
  - ☐ Once a month, take everything out and wipe down fridge. (30 minutes)

- **Friday: slush day (use this to catch up)**
  - ☐ If you missed a zone, do that one on Friday.

    ☐ You can also use this day for deep-cleaning tasks, like mopping or cleaning the fridge.

    ☐ If you notice dirty spots during the week, make a note where you can see it—you can work on it Friday.

With this schedule you don't have to clean on weekends. If you would rather clean on the weekend, you can shuffle these zones around to include Saturday and Sunday and remove your busiest weekdays from the cleaning schedule.

WORKING AT HOME

I do not use the phrase "staying at home" because "working at home" is a better description. Paid or unpaid, our work matters. If you are home, there is more flexibility for your cleaning schedule. You can break it up over the day and do not have the pressure to finish it before or after a commute. That said, I find that cleaning immediately in the morning is most convenient (and I can't procrastinate as easily as I can later in the day). On days I have commitments outside of the house—Mondays we're at homeschool co-op all morning, and Thursdays I work outside the home all day—we either do the cleaning early in the morning before leaving, or do it after dinner for twenty minutes, as in the previous schedule.

The following schedule is what we've used for the last four years. Note: I combine living room/dining/kitchen because they're all on the main floor and get the most traffic; I also do these twice a week. You could break these up across the week or combine as you see fit.

- **Monday: living room and kitchen or main space**
  - ☐ Vacuum all floors, including edges. (10–15 minutes)
  - ☐ Dust/wipe surfaces. (5–10 minutes)

☐ Remove pillows and blankets, then vacuum sofa. (5 minutes)

☐ Wash windows. (5 minutes)

- **Tuesday: bathrooms**
  ☐ Wipe down toilet (can use Lysol wipes in a pinch). (3 minutes)

  ☐ Sweep floor. (3 minutes)

  ☐ Dump trash into kitchen bin. (2 minutes)

  ☐ Wash sink and mirror. (5–7 minutes)

  ☐ Spray and scrub shower (I usually do this on Friday or as needed). (30 minutes)
    - My kids love cleaning bathrooms (what a gift; I don't!) and split the tasks among themselves. My toddler son wipes counters and my daughters split the toilets and sinks. I wash mirrors.

- **Wednesday: bedrooms**
  ☐ Shake out curtains and dust curtain rod/walls. (5 minutes)

  ☐ Vacuum floor; move nightstands and use hose to vacuum edges and under bed. (10 minutes)

  ☐ Wipe off flat surfaces. (10 minutes)

  ☐ Every day: make bed, air out room (window open for 10 minutes), put clothes in hamper, pick up toys/items on floor. (15–20 minutes)

- **Thursday: living room and kitchen (main space)**
  ☐ Vacuum all floors, including edges. (10–15 minutes)

  ☐ Dust/wipe surfaces. (5–10 minutes)

  ☐ Remove pillows and blankets, then vacuum sofa. (5 minutes)

  ☐ Sort/arrange any toy baskets or books. (5–10 minutes)

  ☐ Wash windows. (5–10 minutes)

  ☐ Once every two weeks, mop floors. (30–60 minutes)

   • Note: the second day we clean the main floor, I have more time, so I do a more thorough cleaning.

• **Friday: deep-clean day**

  ☐ Spot-clean areas that escaped notice earlier in the week:

   • laundry room

   • showers

   • entryway

   • refrigerator

   • playrooms

  ☐ Or, if you missed a day, bump that day's cleaning to Friday!

• **Note:** We do a quick pick up of toys at transitions, usually before meals. I don't consider organization/pickup "cleaning," so that's a separate task integrated naturally into the day. The kids are responsible for putting away toys they used (toddlers can help).

There is no fixed rule for how to go about cleaning a home. There is no official playbook, no right and wrong, other than godly stewardship of what we've been given. And stewardship is not legalistic, performance-based effort. It is gracious, consistent, and peaceful. When we arrive at biblical stewardship, we find ourselves not burdened but *blessed* by the systems we've created.

What's the whole point, though? What we do one week is undone by the end of it. This "undoing" is caused by life: heart-throbbing, laughter-inducing, beautiful, hilarious, lovely, precious life. You could have a house that never undid your work; it would be called a museum, and few go to a museum to feel loved. If you want to be truly alive, you must accept some undoing as evidence of life well-lived. In the dirt that accumulates on our washed floors, the dishes that stack back up at each meal, and the dust that gathers on picture frames, we are called to serve the people who live with us and who visit us. We can lay before them a cared-for home, an expression of how seriously we take God's glory; the way His goodness manifests through four walls and a table. The mess is an undoing, yes, but it is a beautiful one.

It's just a cleaning schedule . . . but not really. It's a spiritual discipline. It's a choice to honor the place we live, to free ourselves to experience more peace, to feel confident opening our door to people in need. It's a discipline leading to freedom: freedom from clutter, freedom from constant labor, freedom to spend more time in the Word or prayer or heart-to-heart with friends. It's just a cleaning schedule. But not really. It's a pattern of doing again what has been undone, so we—like our Father—can pick up the pieces of a life well-loved.

A Liturgy for Cleaning

Oh, Lord God:
You know what it is like to make someone clean,
to see that work undone within a day.
Yet You bend again and again
offering all of Yourself for our purity.
Am I too good for the work You do?
Is cleaning up after people too good for me?
You show me the way of humility;
the God who was not too proud to kneel,
to wear the dirt of the earth on His sandals,
to be born in a manger—
is the same God who calls me to kneel
in service of the people around me,
to scrub, to wash, to dust, to clean.
And when what I have done is dirty once again
help me remember Your grace,
that I may give it abundantly to others.
Amen.

CHAPTER 10

Wash on Monday

The Liturgy of Laundry

LAST WINTER, AS THE SNOW PILED UP IN POWDERED-sugar mounds around our house, we read aloud from *Little House in the Big Woods*. The first in the well-beloved Laura Ingalls Wilder series is best read, teachers say, in the winter of a child's fifth year. Laura is five in the story, and Eva was five when we read it. Though our life looks far different from Laura's, some of the home routines were familiar—like this poem Ma Ingalls quotes to her daughters as they go about the daily chores:

> Wash on Monday,
> Iron on Tuesday,
> Mend on Wednesday,
> Churn on Thursday,
> Clean on Friday,
> Bake on Saturday,
> Rest on Sunday.[1]

Little House illustrates just how much work it was to simply survive: making every meal from ingredients you grew, harvested, preserved, and stored, or raised and processed; making your own clothes, outdoor wear, blankets, and furniture. The sheer amount of work is overwhelming to read about and makes me grateful for the privileges I have today. Despite the differences, we can learn from Ma Ingalls's process. To manage the workload, she batched her tasks. By consolidating types of labor to specific days (or in my case, dividing labor into smaller chunks over the course of the week), she provided for her family with skill.

Ma divided her laundry duties into ironing and washing. Her washing routine would have included hauling water from the creek, heating it over a fire, scrubbing the clothes on a metal washboard in the water, then hanging them to dry. The next day she would iron the clothes with weighted metal irons heated in the fire, used to press out the wrinkles. Is this making our modern laundry routines a little more appealing? It is for me!

What was a matter of survival and having clothes to wear (Laura and her family would not have had five work dresses or abundant pairs of socks; they had to do laundry on schedule to clothe themselves) is still a recurring responsibility in today's age. Even with our conveniences, we still do the work of pioneers. How we choose to see the daily or weekly movements from washer to dryer to folding to dresser can be purposeful, and even joyful.

Jesus said in Matthew 6:27–29: "And which of you by being anxious can add a single hour to his span of life? And why are you anxious about clothing? Consider the lilies of the field, how they grow: they neither toil nor spin, yet I tell you, even Solomon in all his glory was not arrayed like one of these." Jesus' point was God's provision. We are not the ones providing for ourselves, God is. God has supplied our needs down to the clothes we wear. Every time we do laundry we experience a physical reminder of God's abundant provision for our needs. Each dishcloth we fold, each pair of socks we match, each pair of pants we stack tunes our hearts to His kindness. The lilies of the field simply grow, clothed in the beauty God gave them. They aren't pressured by influencers to look better, buy more, be newer or trendier. Their beauty stands the test of time. What if we allowed our laundry to do a work in our hearts? What if that stack of unmatched socks was evidence of God's care?

I mention unmatched socks because they are a test of my patience and my materialism. When the pile gets big, I want to just throw them in the trash and start over. The slowness of the task, the menial nature of it, makes me want to throw in the towel (or, I guess, the sock). But when I view this task as evidence of God's provision for my family, my attitude changes. When I see folding the laundry as proof of God's presence with my family, I can do it with joy. Yes, I'm redoing something done before. I'm washing what was washed last week. But isn't that how God is? He washes away sins we should have overcome by now. He folds us in His arms after folding us in last week, and the week before. He does things again and again with unchanging consistency. We don't see this faithfulness as mundane; we trust it as security. Laundry reminds me that repetition is not always a bad thing. Sometimes it's a symbol of grace.

LOVE AND LAUNDRY

Josh and I split most household tasks. We both work from home for set office hours, leading a team of about ten employees while co-homeschooling our children. I homeschool and handle some household tasks in the morning; he teaches math, does administrative work, and sometimes makes dinner in the afternoon (at the writing of this book, we traded back to me making dinners). With our division of labor, I handle most of the laundry and cleaning. One of our "trades," as we call them, is bedtime routine for laundry. He puts the kids to bed most nights; I handle the mountain of clothes.

There are five of us, so with workout clothes, farm attire, towels, rags, and daily wear the hamper is never empty. But rather than resent this constant task, I found a system for managing it. As with all household tasks, the daily call to stewardship is a reminder of a spiritual reality. Folding clothes is one of my least favorite tasks, but it is a tangible reminder of God's abundant grace. And if a liturgy is a physical act directing the heart to worship, laundry is a liturgy for me: a liturgy of God's providing love. God provides not just clothing but the wisdom to manage it well. There are many ways to do this, but here are a few—starting with what I call the "little every day" option.

Lisa Jacobson

Lisa is what I call a "frentor": a friend/mentor. Lisa is a pastor's wife, mother to eight adult children (including a sweet daughter with special needs), grandmother, author, and podcaster. What can't Lisa do?! I'll never forget the day I learned what Lisa loves to do—laundry. Naturally, I wanted to offer up all my laundry for consideration. When I asked her why she liked it, she had a fascinating reply: "Honestly, I love the imagery of washing and going from dirty to clean," she said. "On a more practical level, I truly love blessing my family with clean, folded clothes. And my husband and kids have come to realize that it really is a gift from me, and they truly appreciate it . . . from my hands and heart." Lisa even makes the process more enjoyable by using detergent in scents she loves and taking special care to launder according to directions. Bonus: she always looks put together. Maybe evidence of how the liturgy of laundry pays off?

THE LITTLE-EVERY-DAY PLAN

My goal is to avoid laundry on the weekend. I have friends to see, outdoor tasks to do, work to catch up on, and books I want to read. There are weekends when laundry is necessary (we got sick; we fell behind; we missed a day), but as a general rule, the little-every-day plan keeps the mountain of clothing at bay! Here's how to create your own plan.

Write down all the types of laundry you do:

- sheets, towels, rags
- cloth diapers (I did this—I was a glutton for punishment)
- work uniforms or scrubs
- dresses, blouses, undergarments
- jeans and heavy shirts/sweatshirts
- kids' clothes

Once you have your list, divide the categories into five sections. You'll do one section each weekday (or day of the week, with a catch-up/blank day wherever you want it on your calendar). Here is how ours turned out:

Monday: sheets/towels/rags
Tuesday: adult clothes (gentle/delicate)
Wednesday: kids' clothes
Thursday: adult clothes (heavy duty)
Friday: catch-up day

I limit myself to one load of laundry a day. We might run an extra load if someone is sick or a stain gets on a couch cover; there are pick-up loads here and there. But as a general rule, one load a day from start to finish is enough to keep the five of us on top of the laundry. Our oldest child (age eight at the time of writing) does her own, so on that day we run two loads, but she is in charge of folding.

Typical protocol is to divide by light and dark, which keeps newer clothes from leaching dye on your lighter shirts. I confess after the first wash I get a little lax on this; instead I sort by clothing *weight* and whose it is. For instance, I don't wash lightweight shirts with jeans or towels. Linens and towels are washed together, so they don't ruin finer textures. Jeans and sweatshirts are washed on their own (some would wash jeans completely by themselves; others claim you can *freeze* them, in the freezer! I have never tried this). A few more tips:

- Laundry cleans best if it can move around in the washer, so don't overfill it.
- Sorting clothes by weight and/or quality ensures their longevity and allows you to customize the wash setting to their needs; for instance, Permanent Press for delicate shirts, Heavy Duty for jeans or towels.
- Socks can be put in a mesh bag so you don't lose them to the fourth dimension.
- Turn stinky items (workout clothes, uniforms) inside out for a better clean. You can also do this with dark items.
- Tie drawstrings so they don't tangle, and snap bra straps together or put them in a mesh bag (for really nice lingerie, hand-wash and hang dry).
- Pair folding laundry with a favorite podcast, playlist, or TV show.

If you have older children, they can be taught to do their own laundry to take some of the load off parents' plates. This reduces sorting time when you fold and put away! But even if you have little children, I've found that doing laundry by *person* rather than *color* makes putting away much easier. The whole basket goes to one individual—they put it away, and done! (I realize by ignoring the color requirement, I am offending some of your sensibilities, but it works for us.)

The key here is to start the load immediately upon waking (especially if you leave for work early) and switch it to the dryer when done, then fold at night and put it away at bedtime. There are days I don't get to the folding and putting away, so I roll it to the next day. There is grace for that.

THE ALL-AT-ONCE PLAN

This is the *Little House on the Prairie* "Ma Ingalls" plan. Rather than do a little each day, you can dedicate one whole day just to laundry—nothing else. I have an aversion to housework on weekends, plus our family is committed to rest on Sundays (an intentional choice, and sacrifice, to trust God with our time), so I try to do my work throughout the week. But maybe you actually prefer the "all at once" method or it's the better choice with your work schedule. If so, here are a few ways to make this a bit less daunting:

- If you have kids, involve them. Littles can fold washcloths and build cloth "towers." Let them learn with you now. They can also toss clothes in the washer and dryer, pour detergent, and add laundry sheets.
- Still sort by weight. This is better for your clothes and is more efficient for putting away; plus, you can easily see which load you're doing and check off the list as you go!
- Set timers for when the loads will be done so you can switch them into the dryer right away, and hang dry anything made of linen, wool, silk, or as designated on the tag. (You can use a folding drying rack or you can buy a retracting indoor clothes wire.)
- Fold clothes while they are still warm so they don't have time to wrinkle. Designate a spot to fold; I use my living room floor.
- Try sorting the items before you fold. I either sort by person or by clothing type (but if I sort by type, I have to re-sort by person).

- Set aside any items you need to iron. I like to do these all at once in the evening while I watch a show.

Whichever plan you choose, ask yourself: Is this facilitating more joy in my home? Can I learn to see God's hand in something as simple as laundry—while making practical choices to ease some of the load?

I return again and again to the act of wash, dry, fold, put away— wishing someone would do it for me on occasion. But in doing it over and over, watching baby clothes grow to toddler clothes grow to little girl clothes, I learn something in the repetition. I learn the rhythm of gratitude. I learn to observe God's provision in the repetition. On my knees on the living room floor, piling up washcloths, I pile up prayers of thanksgiving for the goodness of a God who also saw mundane acts as worship.

I may sound like a broken record, but it's worth saying again: no routine is a savior in itself. Routines are not the point; the point is a gentle discipline leading to freedom. Most people do not want to be captive to a pile of laundry on the weekend. They want to be free, and little disciplines during the week, small acts of dedication and stewardship—based on an eternally minded purpose—free us to enjoy our lives in the midst of recurring tasks. Laundry isn't exciting, but it's necessary. And God does not look down on any task that can be done to display His goodness.

A LITURGY FOR LAUNDRY

Lord Jesus:
As we wash and dry, hang and fold the clothes we're blessed to wear,
remind us of the lilies: they do not toil or spin.
They do not strive, but You clothe them.
I need not worry about having more time.
I need not give in to resentment for this holy task.
As I kneel before You, folding, may my heart unfold
before You, willing to see the beauty here
and the truth You are forming in me.
May this act of faithfulness, a gratitude for Your provision,
be a daily and weekly reminder
that You will clothe me without my striving
and all my needs are met in You.
Amen

CHAPTER 11

A Watered Garden

The Liturgy of Tending and Mending

IN THE BEGINNING, WHEN GOD INVENTED WORK AND delegated some of it to His children, work was pleasant and beautiful. It didn't take much for the world to respond to Adam's touch. There was nothing prickly or resistant to his tending. The earth blossomed and flourished with the care of God's people.

Work may have changed because of sin's effects, but one thing remains from Eden: we are still tending people. I find it fascinating that so many people enjoy gardening. I am intrigued by the return to homesteading and so-called self-sufficient living. Our culture has progressed so far, it's like we're going back to our roots—back to centuries of hands in the dirt, plants being watered, fruit being grown. Sometimes it's in the kitchen window, sometimes it's on a stretch of land; but in both, we return to a garden.

In between the daily tasks—the must-dos of dishes, cleaning, laundry, and meals—are less regular tasks that still require attention. They're bigger, more complicated, and sometimes disruptive to our routines. They aren't regular enough to be integrated into the daily maintenance of the home, but they still need to be done.

I call these "tending tasks." They include things like gardening (which is seasonal), ironing, mending, outdoor work, car maintenance, and bigger home projects like renovations. These tasks balloon beyond their limits and threaten to drown us, especially when we don't yet have systems for all the daily things we have to do.

But tending tasks, interruptive as they are, remind me most of God's gardener heart. I have a soft spot in my heart for green things—perhaps because my first job was in a greenhouse. The garden designer, in his heyday, had been the gardener at a world-famous hotel. I loved to listen to him talk: how he described planting flowers in sun or shade based on their species, how to arrange them so they complemented one another or attracted bees, how he created vibrant floral displays in each season of the year. He even taught me how to graft one fruit tree onto another (anyone reminded of Romans 11?). From listening to him, I learned that the best gardeners are *patient*. They tend and wait, tend and wait, hoping their work will bear fruit.

God also tends and waits. He plants, waters, prunes, guards, and harvests. The whole Bible is full of this agricultural terminology. One of my favorite passages is in John 15: "I am the true vine, and my Father is the gardener. He cuts off every branch in me that bears no fruit, while every branch that does bear fruit he prunes so that it will be even more fruitful" (vv. 1–2 NIV).

Cutting a plant you've grown, worked for, and babied feels terrible at the time. If you've ever cut back a perennial flower, you know how it feels! The leftover plant looks small and forlorn. But the next year, that plant will sprout new growth and be more lovely than before. God also prunes us: cutting off the old so the new can bloom and be fruitful. But even in the process of cutting us back, He never leaves us; we are always attached to the vine of Jesus Christ. Our ability to bear fruit is a credit to God Himself, because without Him we can do nothing (John 15:5). God makes a cut, knowing our attachment to Christ will heal it, and out of that wound we will grow more vibrant, beautiful, and life-giving than before.

Which brings me to the other part of tending tasks: mending tasks. What God tends, He mends. After the fall, the brokenness of the world deserved immediate punishment. But God gave grace. He stitched together a story, hope for a Redeemer, promised on the cusp of the curse. Out of this terrible fall would come a bright morning star (Revelation 22:16). The tear in God's relationship with humanity would be mended, not by man but by God Himself.

God loves broken things. He does not love that they are broken, nor does He break them Himself; He permits us the choices we make. Then He offers His whole heart to put us back together:

- "The Lord is near to the brokenhearted and saves the crushed in spirit" (Psalm 34:18).
- "He heals the brokenhearted and binds up their wounds" (Psalm 147:3).
- "The sacrifices of God are a broken spirit; a broken and contrite heart, O God, you will not despise" (Psalm 51:17).
- "For thus says the One who is high and lifted up, who inhabits eternity, whose name is Holy: 'I dwell in the high and holy place, and also with him who is of a contrite and lowly spirit, to revive the spirit of the lowly, and to revive the heart of the contrite'" (Isaiah 57:15).

God sees value in our brokenness. He picks us up, restores us, and makes us new. Each time we repent and turn toward Him we have an opportunity to walk more confidently in our righteous identity. He is with those who are lowly, who can't make it without Him tending to them.

When I think about God's tending and mending Spirit, it gives an eternal value to these inconvenient tasks. So when I'm picking up sticks in the yard, I'm not just stewarding the place He's given; I'm echoing the heart of a Father who bends to fix what the storm destroyed.

THE RHYTHM OF
TENDING AND MENDING

Tending and mending are those "as needed" tasks that are very dependent on lifestyle and your weekly schedule. Not all of us will have (or want to have) a garden; not all of us know how to sew, darn, knit, or fix things around the house. But chances are we know how to do *some* of these things, and some of the others we can learn. Many of us also live with roommates or spouses whose skills complement ours, and together we repair what is broken.

Tending tasks, in the Masonheimer home, fall on weekends or Fridays. Smaller mending jobs like sewing on a button, stitching a torn shirt, or fixing a broken toy can be done during family time in the evening. Sometimes I'll make a pile of mending tasks over the course of a month and work on them while we watch a movie. I can sew a little, but I am terrible at fixing toys. That's where Josh comes in. He's the miracle worker of broken things. If he can't glue it or put it back together, he finds a new way to mend it.

Why fix something if you can just buy new? Stewardship and patience. In this consumer culture, we are quick to throw things away and get something new. In some cases, that's necessary. But taking care of our things teaches us appreciation and patience, an act of stewardship for the money we spent (or that others spent on us). Our children learn from this. They learn you can't just buy something new if you break what you have; you're responsible to care for the things God lends to you, to tend and mend them, to care for them out of gratitude for God's provision. And when we learn to care for our belongings out of a deep, abiding theology of stewardship, our items last longer. This applies to toys and clothes but also to our homes as a whole. Just because our homes aren't what we wish they were doesn't mean we neglect them. We steward them with the same care we would a dream home, knowing that the skills we use to care for the place God has us are the same skills we will need if we one day move on.

Though we only have a little land (three acres), we have five willow trees, all of which shed their branches through our windy winters. Springtime finds us and the children picking up sticks, raking old apples and walnuts from the fall, and cleaning out the garden to prepare for planting. Tasks like these take several hours, so we break them up over a few weekends. Little children can toss apples in a bucket and get paid a nickel a walnut (this is a favorite, but we reduced the wage from a dime a walnut because the kids were putting us in financial distress).

Tending tasks are difficult because they're out of sight, easily forgotten, and often feel "on top of" everything else. We procrastinate on them, but they're always there—niggling at the back of our minds. Josh and I have found that a master list of farm projects, which we can check off over a three-month period, works best. I've listed our tending tasks below; yours will look very different, so remember this is just an example.

Spring:

- Pick up sticks.
- Rake apples and walnuts.
- Shovel any "gifts" from our dog.
- Rake garden beds.
- Maintain lawn mower.
- Fertilize garden.
- Begin planting in late May.

Summer:

- Mow lawn.
- Weed and tend garden.
- Clean up patio.
- Blow leaves off driveaway.
- Sweep porch and sidewalk.
- Organize animal barns for birthing season.
- Put up fences.

Fall:

- Prep barns for winter.
- Harvest apples and garden.
- Blow and rake leaves.
- Organize garage.

Winter:

- Snow blow and shovel driveway.
- Clean up sticks as needed.
- Car maintenance.
- Interior renovation projects.

Winter is the lightest season in our quarterly model of tending tasks. Our winters actually last more than three months (they last almost six), so the other three seasons are much shorter, which is when we do the bulk of tending work. Josh takes most maintenance or machinery tasks; I take care of the animals and gardening and help with yardwork (along with the kids). Your family or homelife is specific to you, so finding a way to fit these tasks in must be ideal for your situation—not mine or anyone else's. Here are some questions you can ask as you determine how to make a routine for time-consuming but less frequent tasks:

- How often do I need to do this?
- How much time does this take?
- Can I break this into a multistep process? Can I schedule those steps across a few days?
- Which season requires the most "tending tasks"? Can I move anything out of that season and into another lighter one?
- Is there someone in my home or community who could help me complete this task?
- Can I pair this task with something I enjoy, such as a podcast or audiobook? Or talking with a friend?

When we lived in the city, our sidewalks and driveway were conveniently snow- and leaf-blown by the city employees. That was one task off our list. We had other items—like painting our chipped picket fence, fixing the brick patio, and replacing the front door—that found a spot on the list instead. We spaced these out over the months and, in some cases, asked for help (a team of wonderful college students, who we had the privilege of leading for three years, painted our fence in exchange for pizza).

HOPE FOR THE BLACK THUMB

This isn't a book about gardening, but I would be remiss if I didn't mention my journey from black thumb to gardener. Though I've always had an interest in horticulture, I was far too impatient to succeed. I knew a lot from books (I even took a semester-long Master Gardening class), but practically, I just wasn't diligent or patient enough to check every day, get my nails dirty, and give the plants what they needed to thrive. My first garden was in the two raised beds of our shady, picket-fenced backyard. It was a beautiful yard, and the shade was great in summer—unless you were trying to grow plants! The house even came with a giant aboveground composter. I thought I was good to go. Just plant the plants, water, and voila! You're a gardener.

It was a little more complicated than that. I didn't want to come out every day to check the plants, but my absences allowed slugs, snails, and squirrels to undo what I accomplished when present. Even my efforts at composting resulted in little more than discovering an entire carton of eggs, intact, in the compost container (if you've ever wondered how bad a rotten egg really smells, trust me—it's not worth finding out).

I gave up after that year and didn't try again until we moved to the farm. This time I had the opposite problem: our garden was in the sun for twelve hours a day. On top of this our well has a habit of running out of water at the twenty-minute mark. Wherever water is being used—sink, toilet, shower, washing machine, dishwasher, or garden sprinkler—when the water runs out, it *runs out*. We don't have water anywhere until it fills back up twenty or so minutes later. As one might guess, this makes gardening in full sun difficult.

Even with these challenges, I tried my hand at a garden: first one year, then two, then three. By the third year I was growing corn next to my zucchini; strong, red tomatoes; peas that climbed higher than the trellis; and a patch of herbs I could use all winter long. What changed? Nothing, except *me*. I stopped seeing the garden as a project of convenience, as a hobby I could drop. I started seeing it as an expression of stewardship and a place to learn more tangibly the parable of growth. The Bible is full of agricultural symbolism. Most of it was written in agrarian cultures, to people who made a living by working the ground. Many American Christians have moved away from those industries, but gardening returns us to them. When we plant, sow, tend, and reap, we connect to one of the oldest acts humanity has ever bent to do. Through this identification, we see with greater clarity the plant-based metaphors Scripture uses to teach us:

"And the LORD will guide you continually
and satisfy your desire in scorched places
and make your bones strong;
and you shall be like a watered garden,
like a spring of water,
whose waters do not fail." (Isaiah 58:11)

"The kingdom of heaven is like a grain of mustard seed that a man took and sowed in his field. It is the smallest of all seeds, but when it has grown it is larger than all the garden plants and becomes a tree, so that the birds of the air come and make nests in its branches." (Matthew 13:31–32)

Gardening is not required for deep spirituality, but there is evidence that tending plants (whether tending houseplants, a window herb garden, or an in-ground garden in your yard) can reduce "stress, fear, anger and sadness" as well as blood pressure and muscle tension.[1] I can't help but wonder if caring for green things connects us to our origin story and the Creator Himself: the garden and the Gardener. God didn't create the first garden so man and woman could be alone; He created a space for community. Our tending tasks do the same thing. They connect to a deeper mission of treating home as a place of significant value. Like the grain of a mustard seed, we plant seeds of faithfulness in little, unseen tasks, but they grow larger and larger until an entire community can be housed within the branches of the home we've built.

Yes, the tending tasks interrupt us. But they are an interruption leading to growth.

A LITURGY FOR TENDING

Lord our God,
 You are a Gardener. You plant the truth
 in all kinds of soil, knowing well who will receive
 the seed You've cast.
 You know what it's like to see work undone.
 You know what it's like to till hard soil.
 You know what it's like to fix broken things.
 Thank You, O God, for Your patient compassion.
 You do not tire of our brokenness;
 You strive with us, carry us, heal us, and tend us.
 We blossom under Your care.
 May we see our tending tasks with the same compassion,
 may we look at them with purpose,
 and take part in Your mending nature
 when we repair and restore.
 Amen

CHAPTER 12

Filled with the Spirit

The Liturgy of Beauty

THE PICTURE HUNG IN THE CORNER, NEXT TO A ROW OF leather-bound books and a stack of worship CDs: Michael Card, Avalon, 2nd Chapter of Acts. The picture never moved from the corner, that I remember. It was always there, looking out at the living room, easy to capture at a glance. You couldn't help but glance at it—the face in the corner. A happy face, but a presence nonetheless.

It was called *Laughing Jesus*, a loosely sketched drawing of Jesus, head thrown back, laughing for all He was worth (which, as we know, is quite a lot). I loved it. As a young child I stared at it, captured by the smile and upturned face. As an older teen I found comfort in it. It was one of only two Christian art pieces I remember from that home; the other was a painting of a sleeping child with a guardian angel standing over him. That one hangs in the hallway by my children's bedrooms, a quiet testimony to two childhoods: mine and theirs.

The *Laughing Jesus* impacted me so profoundly, I wrote a poem about it:

> He was a laughing Jesus that I knew:
> crow's-feet gathered

at the corners of His eyes,
and in the corners of my heart
I knew that I knew that I knew:
this Jesus liked me.
Why else would He laugh?
There was no brimstone, only fire:
the fire of a love that cannot die
In the eyes of a God who died for love.

He was a laughing Jesus that I knew
and since, I've gathered
as many ears as are willing to hear
in the corners of apps & living rooms
to know that they know that they know:
Jesus likes them.
Why else would He die?

"LAUGHING JESUS," *PDM*

Styles change and architecture alters, but home beautification has less to do with trends and more to do with the culture of faith you're creating within the walls. What do you want to celebrate, elevate, and make visible within your home? What do you want to look at every day? What do you want to be reminded of when you walk into the kitchen or sit on the couch? Decoration is preferential; it is personal, but it is also purposeful. How we beautify our homes tells the story of our life in pictures, art, color, and design.

FILLED WITH THE SPIRIT OF GOD TO MAKE ART

The Bible tells us about a time God inspired art—and not just any art but precious, holy art. Israel was building the tabernacle, their mobile temple. The pattern for these items came directly from God and had to be made with utmost care. God knew exactly who He wanted for the job.

> Then the LORD said to Moses, "See, I have chosen Bezalel son of
> Uri, the son of Hur, of the tribe of Judah, and I have filled him
> with the Spirit of God, with wisdom, with understanding, with
> knowledge and with all kinds of skills—to make artistic designs
> for work in gold, silver and bronze, to cut and set stones, to work
> in wood, and to engage in all kinds of crafts" (Exodus 31:1–5 NIV)

Bezalel was skilled to do metalwork, cut stones, carve wood, and create "all kinds of crafts." Imagine! Perhaps He could knit, crochet, sculpt, and paint. The Bible doesn't say, but it does say the Spirit empowered him with "wisdom . . . understanding . . . knowledge and . . . skills." Creating beauty (emulating God's creative ability) is a gift of the Spirit, empowered by His strength. Not all of us are called to careers in exemplary art, but we can still appreciate and display art that turns the mind toward Christ rather than away from Him.

I don't mean we must decorate our homes in Christian signage; to the contrary, my own home is decorated with beautiful things that don't have any direct connection to Scripture but which reflect the scriptural values of order, intention, goodness, and truth. My favorite gallery wall has a cross-stitch made by my mother, two miniatures of classic American paintings, a collection of postage stamps with horse designs, a watercolor of a covered bridge, and two landscape paintings I made during an attempt at acrylics. There is nothing directly spiritual about this wall, but when I look at it, I experience delight. I love horses, and I love the art piece *Snap the Whip*; the covered bridge reminds me of our engagement, and my paintings—well, they aren't very good, but they're of our farm, and I like them.

Decorating your home is about joy. It's not about comparison. It's not about trends. If you don't like pinning baskets to your walls or hanging a letterboard, don't do it. What do you like? What brings you joy? What could you look at daily and be reminded of God— His heart, His sovereignty, His goodness? I am reminded of God when I look at my little canvas on the wall. Never mind that part of it looks like a kindergartener painted it; there's one part I really like: the clouds. And when I look at those clouds, I see God's kindness. So I leave it on the wall.

One of the places women feel deep shame regarding their homes is in the area of decor. Some believe they simply aren't good at it but should be (I've been there). Others want a specific look but feel it is unachievable. Others have been captured by comparison and materialism, unhappy with any compromise to the vision in their minds. But if creating beauty echoes God's character, and the Spirit particularly equips us for the task, what the world is doing is good for little more than basic inspiration. It cannot dictate how we decorate (or if we decorate at all). Contentment gives us the gift of clarity: What do I actually like? What do I actually think is beautiful, apart from the current trends?

I really like nineteenth century American art. I also like paintings of horses, watercolor landscapes, and lots of texture. I'm not particularly good at understanding scale (making sure furniture is not too large for a room, or art too small for a wall) so I have to sift through photos online to find a look I can copy. But deep in my heart, I know what I am after. I have an idea for the home, a way to make it a little cozier, calmer, and sweeter. The things I like—vintage salt and pepper shakers, chintzy kitchen towels, lots of fluffy pillows, wool throw blankets—might not be "in," but they bring me joy. When added together the house expands beyond what I like, to offer all of itself, in all its hygge glory, to those who enter.

Our goal in beautifying the home should never be to compete

or meet a benchmark. We should look at beautification as a labor of love: What do I love? How can I show what I love on the walls of this home? And if our chief love is Christ, there is a way to weave His truth into our home with tact and beauty. Perhaps it's *Laughing Jesus*. Or maybe it's more subtle than that.

One home we visited kept a little shadow box on the wall by the table. The shadow box contained random items, each with a story of God's faithfulness.

By our piano hang two framed pieces of sheet music, both hymns. They were given to me by a friend: "Be Thou My Vision" and "Amazing Grace," both favorites in our home. They remind me of God's truth.

In the kitchen hangs a picture of Eve and Mary: Eve weeping as a snake winds around her ankle, and Mary comforting her as she crushes its head. It's an image to take your breath away, and it hangs by my piles of dirty dishes, sanctifying their ordinariness.

Whatever you love, let it shine in your home. Whatever way God has met you in your story, *tell that story* so others can ask.

LET ART TELL A STORY

If you feel like you're not good at creating beauty, or are confused about where to begin, ask God. God invented beauty. He created its diversity, and He can guide you into things that bring you joy (He is interested in our joyfulness; it is a fruit of His Spirit). Ask Him to show you the art, music, and design that would make home a blessing to you.

As you await His answer, explore ideas. Ask questions. Think about what colors, shapes, books, and paintings you are drawn to; what about them do you like? Do they evoke an emotion? Do they remind you of an experience? If you've identified a connection, look for similar pieces or patterns and follow the thread.

One of the best tips I received from a friend naturally skilled at decorating is to create a space with different shapes and textures. For instance, don't add too many rectangles to a rectangular room: a boxy sofa, a rectangular coffee table, square pictures on the walls. If you have a boxy sofa, add an oval coffee table, and vary the size of the art on the walls (better yet, group them together in galleries). For texture, I like to thrift baskets of different sizes and hang them in a group ascending my living room wall. It's inexpensive and adds dimension to a large, square room.

In the bathroom I hung two paintings I love: one is of our first house, the cottage in town. The other is a watercolor given to me by my favorite journalism professor. Both have sentimental value and a neutral color with black frames, fitting for the white and green bathroom. The design fits, but I put them there because they tell a story.

This is why I (personally) don't buy art pieces from big-box stores unless there is a significant, meaningful phrase or image. Each piece in our home has meaning. It's part of the Masonheimer legacy; a story we can tell, hidden in pictures. I'm not against commercial art; one of my favorite pieces was bought there. It's a large, scripted piece that says, "The Lord will fight for you; you need only be quiet." My sister bought it when I broke my leg, hung it where I could see it from the sofa, and told me to remember the truth of it until I could walk again. It hangs in our living room, overlooking the stairs, a reminder of a season of true dependence.

Inexpensive art is not always bad, but I encourage you to buy what truly identifies with your story. Look for items that say more than "farmhouse." If someone came and looked around your living room, would there be something they could ask to know more about? A picture of your family, a religious art piece, a church liturgical calendar, a framed Scripture verse, a comforting landscape scene? Choose what you love and let it tell your story.

THE ROTATING ART MUSEUM

Our children have a penchant for artistry, mostly with markers and construction paper. We find half-finished rainbows, spindly princesses, colorful houses, and all manner of silly faces scattered around the house. We wanted to display the best of it in a special way, and finally landed on our "rotating art museum": a wall of picture frames displaying the best of our children's latest works. But to make it a true art experience, we wrote titles and descriptions for each piece and taped them below the paintings. To complete the display, we bought a battery-operated gallery light and hung it above the drawings.

The kids were delighted by this activity. Every few months we switch out the drawings for new ones, change the descriptions, and laugh hysterically at the titles. Guests are often curious to know the inspiration behind *Spiders Crawling on Mom* and *Iron Golem*. Some of the drawings make sense; others make none at all, which makes them all the more interesting.

Another way to integrate art is to host a weekly "hobby night." Every Wednesday is our hobby night: every member of the family can do an activity of their choice that involves zero media or phones. The kids often choose painting, pastels, or drawing. Sometimes we paint with acrylics. The final pieces can be saved and displayed.

THE BALANCE OF
CONTENTMENT AND JOY

Decor is an easy area in which to become discontent with what we own or the skill with which we style it. The answer is not envy, but neither is the answer apathy ("I can't have what I want, so I will do nothing."). If a lovely home would bring you joy, there is no sin in making it lovely. There are ways to do so without breaking the bank. Here are a few ideas:

- Rugs: These can be bought online through local marketplaces for a deal. Make sure your rug is big enough and that either all four feet of your furniture are on it, or just the front two feet. Don't let a rug "float" in front of your couch.
- Mirrors: Mirrors reflect light and can make a space feel bigger. Framed mirrors look more put together and can be thrifted easily.
- Arranging: Make your sofa "talk" to your chairs. Have them face each other so guests can converse easily. Move them closer together if necessary.
- Resist pushing furniture against the wall: Sometimes this is inevitable, but if you can leave some space, do! It actually makes a room look bigger.
- Hang art to scale: The middle of a picture should be at eye level or sixty to sixty-two inches off the floor. If you do a gallery, you can go higher, but start with your primary piece at eye level and work around it. (A nice trick for hanging: Trace your frames on parchment paper and tape to the wall where you want them. Make a mark for where the nails need to go.)
- Hang curtains higher: To create the illusion of height, order longer curtains and raise the rod almost to the ceiling. It will seem as if the windows extend to where the curtains begin.
- Layer lights, blankets, and textures: Table lamps offset overhead light and make a room feel warmer; a variety of blankets in the same shade but varied textures are comforting for cozy nights; baskets for toys, pillows, and books add color and texture where needed (as well as function).

These tricks cost little but go a long way to bring a home together. This year we found a new-to-us sofa—the first we've had in almost seven years—that perfectly blends with the style of my living room rug and chairs. But for the last seven years we had a different sofa, well-loved and beautiful in its own way, which sent the design of the space an entirely different direction. Both sofas were good. Both served their purpose. I like the new one more, but I was content with the previous one. I did my best to make the old one beautiful and it brought me joy. The new one brings me joy in a new way. How kind is God!

CREATING BEAUTY . . . FOR WHAT?

Bezalel was equipped to create beauty for the purpose of worship. As Christians under the new covenant in Christ, we are created to point to God and direct people to give Him glory. Our homes are a vehicle of this mission. No one is saying we must decorate our homes like a church, but if creating beauty is a work of the Spirit (not just personality or preference), we should create it with worship in mind.

When I decorate my home, I am asking myself: *How does this tell God's story through my life? If someone enters my home, are they pointed to Christ by being present here? Is there a sense of peace, calm, and beauty emanating from this space, or is it chaotic, disorderly, and anxiety-inducing?*

I want people to enter our home and feel drawn to worship: to lift their eyes to God, be reminded of His faithfulness, and feel His presence through our peace. Not all of that can be accomplished through how we steward our home, but much of it can. And the beauty we create here is a gift, not just to us but to those who need hope that good things still thrive in the land of the living.

A LITURGY FOR BEAUTY

Jesus, Creating God:
You gave Beauty her name.
You saw the first sunrise and designed every one since.
You raised the mountains, lowered the valleys,
and traced each morning blade of grass with dew.
You know beauty like the back of Your nail-scarred hand;
it is rare, and good, and available to all.
Help us look for what is true, good, and beautiful,
not just what is new, cool, and trendy.
Set our eyes on things above, where You are,
and shape our tastes to what is truly lovely.
May our homes reflect Your creation
and our lives be an imprint of Your fingers,
a testimony to how amazing grace
makes all things beautiful in their time.
Amen

CHAPTER 13

A Longer Table

The Liturgy of Hospitality

THE SNOW PILES ON THE WINDOWSILL, NEARLY OBSCUR-
ing the view of gray-blue trees rolling away from the cow field.
Everything is pure white or dark slate, from the apple tree still
bobbing leftovers from fall to the barn coated by blasts from the
western wind. Outside, the snow is torrential, but inside is glow-
ing with warmth. Votive candles flicker on the mantel and wool
blankets are tossed on chairs. Floor pillows sit in a stack and a cutting board of crackers and cheese lies waiting for attention on the
ottoman. My oldest daughter is quietly puttering in the kitchen,
making up a packaged brownie mix for our coming guests.

All seasons are good seasons for company, but I like winter
best. Schedules are slower, evenings are darker, and no one wants
to be outside in the blackness. A Monday night invitation is enough
to bring us together over Gouda and raspberries, opening Bibles,
scratching out our thoughts about God and Scripture, sharing
what the Lord has done in our lives to the encouragement of all
listening.

HGTV calls it "entertaining," but the Bible calls it hospitality. There's a stark difference between these two practices. Entertaining says, *"Here I am!* Look at my house, look at my yard, look at my television-worthy display!" Hospitality says, *"There you are!* Look at you, coming here! Come and be welcome! Come and be safe!"

God cares about hospitality. It is commanded (not just implied) multiple times in the Bible, starting with the Mosaic law in Leviticus all the way through the New Testament epistles. One of the very first acts of the Christian church—described in Acts 2:46—was "breaking bread in their homes," cultivating a community of welcome. Here are a few additional verses to illustrate this theme:

- Hebrews 13:2: "Do not neglect to show hospitality to strangers, for thereby some have entertained angels unawares."
- 1 Peter 4:9: "Show hospitality to one another without grumbling."
- Leviticus 19:34: "You shall treat the stranger who sojourns with you as the native among you, and you shall love him as yourself, for you were strangers in the land of Egypt: I am the LORD your God."
- Romans 12:13: "Contribute to the needs of the saints and seek to show hospitality."

But what does the Bible mean when it uses this word? It can't mean what the HGTV channel tells us. The Greek word for "hospitality" is *philóxenos*.[1] It means to love strangers and be generous to guests. Love and generosity do not mark the home renovation industry. Most of what we see is meant to make us envious, driving us to materialism and greed. But true hospitality is not interested in expanding a home "so that" we can host; true hospitality chooses love *today*, in the imperfect house with the little table and a stack of pizza boxes.

Another distinction between God's hospitality and the entertainment industry's is the guest list. Entertaining is about inviting your friends: the people you're comfortable with or want to impress. While inviting friends is a great baseline, it's the minimum in God's expectation. God wants us to love strangers, foreigners, sojourners, *people without a place to call home.* I believe God articulates this command in Scripture because He wants every person to know they have a place with Him, and His people are *the physical manifestation of such a place.* When we open our doors to those in need, we show them what life in Christ looks like. We get to display the love of God through the tangible realities of food, drink, light, a warm blanket, and intentional conversation.

One of the ways my husband and I practice hospitality to strangers is by keeping our eyes and hearts open to spontaneous invitations. I work outside my home office two or three times a week, usually in a downtown coffee shop. Sometimes I fall into a great conversation with someone who is new to the area, or a fellow business owner, and take that opportunity to invite them to dinner that evening. Other times I meet a mom of young children and invite her to a playdate on the weekend to connect her with other women. One of the sweetest memories I have is when we invited a Jehovah's Witness couple, who had come to our door several times, to join us for dinner. Over dinner we exchanged our respective theological views. As the couple left, they thanked us, but also informed us that in fifteen years of going door-to-door this was the first time anyone had asked them to dine.

If you think your little house, humble and small, isn't good enough to invite others in, think about this: many people grow up in homes more beautiful than yours, but the family within it is fractured. There is no love. There is no generosity. There is only pain. Proverbs 17:1 says, "Better a dry crust with peace and quiet than a house full of feasting, with strife" (NIV). This verse became real to me when I worked a job that required me to live onsite in a wealthy neighborhood for several weeks. I had a small room in the giant house, ate all my meals in the kitchen, and occasionally joined the family for dinner, governess-style. I'd never seen so much wealth up close. I got to see other things up close too: Anger. Resentment. Betrayal. Distrust. I left far less envious than before, and far more grateful for my loving family.

Many of the strangers who need our love grew up in houses like this one—full of strife, chaos, and anxiety. These people would rather have your dry-crusted pizza in a house full of peace and joy and quiet and goodness than all the feasting a mansion can offer. Let them in—in the door, in your life. Hospitality is never about us. It's about loving others the way God does.

WE ARE NOT MADE FOR ISOLATION

When God created humans, He created them for relationship. We often turn to Genesis 1–2 to understand marriage, but God's creation of man and woman was not just about sex and procreation. It was also about community. Marriage is a community of two, but it lays the foundation—through children and families—for a community stretching beyond the bounds of blood relation. God's triune nature is communal, and He created people in His image—with an echo of His attributes. We need community. We are not made for isolation, and research backs this up.

God said, "It is not good for the man to be alone" (Genesis 2:18 NIV). According to a meta-analysis by professor of psychology Julianne Holt-Lunstad: "Lack of social connection heightens health risks as much as smoking 15 cigarettes a day or having alcohol use disorder. . . . Loneliness and social isolation are twice as harmful to physical and mental health as obesity."[2] The Survey Center on American Life found that "Nearly one in five Americans reported having no close social connections, a double-digit increase from

2013. And young men are faring worse than most: More than one in four (28 percent) men under the age of 30 reported having no close social connections."[3] This survey defined "close connection" as being able to reach out to someone about a deeply personal issue in the last six months. One in five people could not talk to anyone about their life . . . for at least six months. How heartbreaking!

Being alone is not good for us. We are not made for it. But unless we are intentional about seeking community, will we choose what is easy and convenient: scrolling our phones, isolated from loving and being loved while reading about it online.

Forming community is hard work; we must risk being hurt. But when we refuse to risk hurt, we miss out on great reward. Like C. S. Lewis said in *The Four Loves*:

> To love at all is to be vulnerable. Love anything, and your heart will certainly be wrung and possibly be broken. If you want to make sure of keeping it intact, you must give your heart to no one, not even to an animal. Wrap it carefully round with hobbies and little luxuries; avoid all entanglements; lock it up safe in the casket or coffin of your selfishness. But in that casket—safe, dark, motionless, airless—it will change. It will not be broken; it will become unbreakable, impenetrable, irredeemable.[4]

What is more vulnerable than opening your home? When you allow someone in your house, you're giving them a glimpse of the real you. What most people forget is that vulnerability begets vulnerability. When someone is permitted to enter your space and finds that space a loving place to rest, there is room for them to open something else: their heart.

Karen Ehman

Karen, or Kit, as I know her, is an inspiration to hospitality. An empty nester now, Kit learned to open her home creatively when her kids were still small. Her ideas are innovative and out of the box, adapting hospitality to her season. When I told her I didn't know how to juggle opening our home and also spending time with my husband, she suggested trading date nights with another couple. "When it's their turn to go out, have the kids over to play with each other while you and Josh watch from the couch," she suggested. "You're blessing another couple, welcoming their kids, and then later in the month you'll have a turn to go out." She also suggested easy ways to have people over on a budget: coffee and dessert, potlucks, or backyard barbecues. Kit's desire to bless others made her creative in how she hosted families in all seasons of life. She didn't retire from hospitality as she got older—she just got more creative. Inspiring!

THE COST OF COMMUNITY

After our church's first service on Sunday mornings, we walk next door to the playground. Six of our best couple-friends and their families usually gather here so the children can play. As they swarm the slides and swings, we talk about the cost of community: what it takes to stay in fellowship and to form lasting friend groups. We've been doing this for years, some years with better success than others, and have learned a thing or two about walking with people for the long haul. Josh and I realize the friend group we have is what most people dream of, and we don't have it because we're special. There is so much grace given and received, so much patience on the part of our friends. So much showing up, listening, bearing one another's burdens, celebrating, joking, and growing together.

We all want to be known, to have "our people," to go deep with a group of Christians who know God for real—but so many of us forget the cost. One of my best friends has been by my side for almost seven years. Through those years, we had each other, but forming a larger community was far more difficult. Unreciprocated hosting, uncomfortable coffee dates, try-and-fail friendships, small groups that began and then ended, relationships that drifted apart—these are all part of our story. We often think back on those years and joke that it felt like rolling a boulder uphill!

Community is work, but it's much harder work when it's unreciprocated. I wonder: Would we solve some of this reciprocation problem (which is a universal experience for many American Christians) if we all committed to be reciprocatory people? If we took some initiative, made space in the calendar, answered the text instead of ghosting them? Not everyone will become a best friend. Not everyone is meant to be in the inner circle. But to get an inner circle, you have to have an outer circle. And to get an outer circle, you have to get uncomfortable.

We should come to relationships expecting to do the hard work. If we want community without effort, vulnerability, disagreement, and accountability, we can't have community. Real relationships require grace—what Dr. Henry Cloud and Dr. John Townsend call "gifts from the outside."[5] Grace in community looks like:

- discerning when to express opinions and when to control your tongue;
- learning to listen rather than give quick, pat answers;
- understanding that people are imperfect and need time to grow;
- praying for and with people as they walk through hard things; and
- speaking truth with affection, never with condescension.

Graceless people will do one of two things: they will gather friends who think just like they do, or they will have no friends—only acquaintances. Those who gather like-minded friends will frequently lose those relationships when differences arise, because there is no grace for development of character.

But gracious people grow together. They do not place opinions on issues of preference above the love of God. They know when to agree to disagree, when something needs to be addressed, and when to let go. They put the relationship above performative obligations. And their friendships thrive. People want to be around them because they are light and life, like the God they follow.

When we commit to loving others through hospitality, building a community based around home, we lose a little bit of freedom. We're letting go of independence to choose interdependence and vulnerability. Our culture puts freedom above relationships: no boundaries, no commitments, no accountability or confrontation, and in so doing loses any opportunity for deep, formative relationships. Such relationships take time. They take sacrifice:

- turning off the football game to talk with someone over dinner
- limiting extracurricular activities with your kids so you have time to open your door and set an example for your children
- learning to cook, or putting a line in the budget, to make feeding others a priority
- choosing to say no to another night out with coworkers and instead inviting them to your apartment

Maybe you're ready to commit to the sacrifice. You want to start opening your door in obedience to Christ, showing love in this faithful first step. Here is where to start:

- **Prayer:** I prayed for my community faithfully, before I knew them. Pray for the community you desire. Be specific with the Lord—not just for people who share your likes and dislikes but people who share your deepest values and can truly bear your burdens (and whose burdens you can bear). Then keep your eyes open for His answer, which may come in unexpected ways.

- **Reciprocation:** The struggle with reciprocation is universal. When I talk about hospitality on social media, reciprocation is a constant pain point. People either don't respond to invitations or they never invite in return. I have experienced this difficulty for years and I think it is an American culture issue, likely to go unchanged unless we change it ourselves. Here are some tips:

  ☐ First, many people need time to plan their schedule—last-minute invitations often don't work and will result in a higher rejection rate.
  ☐ Invitations should be specific (date, time, expectation) so people respond yes or no.
  ☐ Reciprocation will happen with people who see their need for community and prioritize it, which brings us back to prayer. Pray for people who value this and who reciprocate. Then do what you can, on your end, to facilitate it.

- **Grace:** Legalism is a community killer. When people elevate second- and third-tier theological issues (doctrinal issues that are not central to Christian theology), they can't maintain close friendship. We simply can't have healthy friendships when we're judging people for their decisions. For example, Josh and I home educate; not all of our friends homeschool their children. Not all of us parent the same way; not all of us have the same theological views on end-times or spiritual gifts. But we are united around Christ and our core values for raising kids who love Him and know Him. This grace makes friendship possible and makes up for the areas of difference.

- **Love for God:** Ultimately the unity of the church, and true community, is formed through the Holy Spirit's work in our hearts. He bonds us to one another. As I walked with a friend today, she told me she can almost physically sense when she meets another Christian—before they even open their mouth! I've felt that too. Love for God bonds Christians to one another with a closeness and depth that, once experienced, is impossible to forget.

My encouragement to all who long for community is this: be prepared to do the work and to do it a long time. But pray as hard as you work at it, and watch God be faithful. I've seen Him come through in multiple churches, in multiple states, in all my life stages. He always comes through, often through our obedience and consistency in opening our doors, but also by working in others to bring us all together in the unity of His Spirit. True community will always have a cost: it will cost time, energy, and vulnerability. But it's the best risk you'll ever take.

PRACTICAL TIPS FOR HOSTING

I have been opening my home for many years, including when I moved back home from college and lived with my parents, when I was a single girl with roommates, when I was newly married in a third-floor apartment, when I was a new mom in a Main Street duplex, when I was a mom of two in a 1,400-square-foot cottage, and now here, at our farm. Since being married, Josh and I have partnered in this lifestyle of hospitality.

Life has always been busy. We always have other things to do. We had imperfect spaces and houses and "too small" living areas. No one ever cared that our house didn't look like a magazine photo.

No one cared when we hauled out folding chairs for extra people, when we bumped against each other when setting up a potluck-style dinner in our galley kitchen, or when we were crammed into our tiny living room sitting cross-legged on the floor. They cared about the community, and our house—however small— facilitated that.

If you aren't accustomed to opening your home or you feel overwhelmed with where to begin, let's start by answering some of the most common concerns and questions about opening your home.

1. HOW DO YOU HOST IF YOU'RE AN INTROVERT?

My husband is a stereotypical introvert and I am an ambivert-bordering-on-introvert. I am tired after hosting—I enjoy it, but it definitely takes my energy. God has compassion on human limitations and personalities. He also gives us His Spirit to empower us to obedience. The command to hospitality in Scripture is not and was not personality-specific. If God expects this heart of welcome, then it follows He believes it possible for *all* people to participate in it. We can adapt hospitality to how God made us!

For introverts, hosting will probably work best in smaller groups—one family at a time or one-on-one meetups. My husband has a hard time being heard in small groups and speaking up. We do host large parties a few times a year (fifty to seventy people) but most of our gatherings are twenty or less.

Introverts do need to keep in mind that the goal is not just to re-invite people you know and are comfortable with, but to reach out to those who need community. You can introduce new acquaintances to people you know well; this helps carry the conversation and builds a lasting connection. If you're nervous or new to hosting, it may help to set a date each week as your "hosting day" and rotate among families you know and those you don't know as well. You can also combine these two so that the more well-known family can help carry conversation and make the other one feel welcome.

2. HOW DO I OPEN MY HOME WHEN IT'S SMALL?

First, recognize that most people aren't bothered by small houses; most people *have* small houses. It's the heart that counts—not the size of your home. Even in tight spaces you can rearrange furniture, grab some floor pillows and folding chairs, and make it work. Kids can play in a corner with toys, or utilize spaces like the kitchen if it's nearby. It's not about the size of your home but the size of your heart. People remember how you made them *feel*, not how big your living room was.

Live in a warm climate? Use your yard! Don't have a backyard? Use the front yard! Set up a table and some chairs and a picnic blanket. Or meet at a park. Be a problem solver.

3. DO I HAVE TO COOK? HOW DO I MAKE FOOD ON A TIGHT BUDGET?

While cooking is often cheaper, you certainly don't have to make the food to be hospitable. Buy a couple of pizzas and have the company bring a salad. There are many creative ways to feed a crowd and they don't all require gourmet cooking skills.

That said: cooking *is* a life skill that will help you in the long term, not just in hospitality but also in sticking to a food budget. Have everyone bring a dish to pass. Make a simple meal like burrito bowls—rice, beans, and toppings—with everyone participating. Focus on vegan recipes if meat is too expensive. Chips and salsa are a few dollars. Look up recipes online and make a list of hosting meals for quick reference.

4. HOW DO YOU OPEN YOUR HOME WHILE ALSO PROTECTING YOUR KIDS?

Having had an unsafe person in my home before, this is very important to me and Josh. We want our home to be available for welcome and comfort "for the sojourner" but we also keep a discerning eye on the kinds of people who enter it. We are not only responsible for our children but also for the other people who enter our home trusting it to be a safe space. We are the guardians of this space. Unsafe people who are resistant to accountability are not allowed to disrupt the peace of our home.

If we get the sense (through the Spirit) that a person is emotionally or spiritually unhealthy to the detriment of the others in our home, we meet those people outside the house either one-on-one or as a group in a public place. Josh meets with single men a few times before they are invited around the children. Occasionally we will have people to group events (three to five other families present) in an outdoor setting. This gives more witnesses and accountability.

We teach our kids appropriate language for their body parts, do not permit kids or adults (except parents and their kids) upstairs during hosting events (we have a baby gate), and prayerfully stay aware of any changes in the community/people we are regularly in contact with. Sometimes a tough conversation needs to be had, but better to have a conversation on the front end than to discover the hurt someone caused after the fact.

5. I INVITE PEOPLE, BUT THEY NEVER COME OVER. WHAT AM I DOING WRONG?

A lot of the time the problem lies in *how* the invitation was issued, not who it was issued to. Ask these questions:

- *Is my invite specific and personal?* Don't say: "Stop by sometime when you're in town." Say, "Are you free to come to dinner from five to seven Thursday evening?"
- *Is my invite too vague?* Don't say: "We should get together sometime." Say, "I have ____ open this week, are you free then?"
- *Did I forget to follow up?* (I do this!) Say, "Hey, I wanted to check in about Saturday. Would that work or would you prefer a different day?"

The next question I ask myself is, *If they came here before, how was the experience? What could I do to make it better?* Was conversation flowing, as far as you could help it along? Were the kids utter chaos—do you need to have a parent take turns watching them? Think about what could be improved for a better experience.

Lastly, if you have invited someone multiple times and they continually ghost, say no, or always ask, "Who else is coming?" before saying yes (this is a tactless question—it basically is asking, "Are you worth my time to attend?"), I would stop pursuing them and focus your energy elsewhere.

6. I'M SINGLE! HOW DO I HOST FAMILIES?

Singles have an incredible gift of flexibility (to a degree, of course; you still have commitments!), enabling them to host in unique ways. When I asked my single and empty-nester readers how they lived out a theology of home, it was primarily through hospitality. They hosted Bible studies, young families, other single friends, and generally acted as a connecting point for people who needed to meet one another. If you're hosting families, you might be intimidated—but don't be! Most families don't mind coming to a house that doesn't have all the kid accommodations. It's the thought that counts.

A few tips: Put away anything that is precious to you. Babies don't know better than to grab, and some children have special needs and struggle with impulse control (to parents of older children who are neurotypical: I encourage teaching them to ask permission before touching items, so going to new homes is easier for both parent and host!). You can invest in some secondhand toys for a bin kept in a closet. You can even ask mom friends for ideas and check Goodwill (then clean them up with cleaning spray). Kids love new toys and books. This will help entertain them when they visit. You can also host groups of a mixed-relationship background:

a family and a couple of singles, perhaps. Groups do not need to be in the same stage of life to enjoy one another.

7. I FEEL LIKE MY HOUSE IS NEVER PRESENTABLE ENOUGH TO HOST. WHAT DO I DO?

First, remember that biblical hospitality is not entertaining. Entertaining is about *you*: you being Martha Stewart, you hosting the perfect meal, you having the Pinterest house. There is nothing wrong with a beautiful house, but that's not the point of biblical hospitality. Hospitality is about the other person. It's selfless. And that's incredibly freeing!

When hosting is not about you, it doesn't matter what people think of you or your house. What you're thinking about is them and their experience. You will want to create a home that is at least clean (no dog hair in their food!) but certainly does not have to be perfect. It's much easier to host regularly when you aren't over-whelmed by home management . . . which is where routines come in. They are a gift to you and they also bless others as you walk in the Great Commission.

8. I HAVE NO PROBLEM HOSTING, BUT WHEN I DO, PEOPLE WON'T LEAVE. WHAT DO I DO?

Be specific about your end time on the invite (via text or in person). You can even say why: "We have to put the kids to bed at eight, so we need to be done by then." I would recommend giving yourself a half hour wiggle room in case you get to talking and go past the time frame.

If someone just won't leave even after significant hints, you might have to be straightforward. Stand up and say, "Well, we have to get to bed because of an early start tomorrow. It was so good seeing you. Can we help pack up your things?" It sounds horrible, but sometimes it's necessary. Hospitality and boundaries are not opposites: boundaries allow us to continue hosting without burnout.

9. HOW OFTEN SHOULD I HOST?

That depends on your season. When I'm newly postpartum, I'm not hosting anybody for six weeks at least. In some seasons our home was open three, four, five times a week for coffee dates, Bible studies, and dinners. When I broke my leg in a season of small children, hosting was impossible again for a time. Allow hosting to flex with your season.

I still recommend picking a day a week (it can be moved around if needed) for hosting others. It's a commitment, a reminder to be ready to invite whenever the opportunity arises. I also keep paper plates and cups on hand, plus easy meals in the freezer or a meal list to work from.

10. HOW DO I GET MY SPOUSE ON BOARD?

First and foremost, pray. Ask for God to change their heart and help them see His vision for His people.

Then . . . communicate. Talk through the objections and questions. Look at the suggestions in this section and think about how you can do this in a way that fits your season and lifestyle. It does not have to be complicated, showy, or huge.

11. SMALL TALK WEARS ME OUT. WHAT DO WE TALK ABOUT?

Conversation is a life skill, one that will be helpful in every arena. When you know how to ask a question, change a topic, or think about the person, you are far less likely to be nervous when talking to someone new.

Conversation is surprisingly simple when we look at it through the lens of selflessness. When we stop thinking about ourselves and instead focus on the other person, questions come more naturally.

Their response to you is not what matters; what matters is your desire to make them welcome. If they are awkward or difficult about your welcome, that is their responsibility, not yours. Focus on welcoming them and give the rest to the Lord.

Ask basic questions if you're new to a person: "What is keeping you busy these days?" "Where are you from?" Then build on their answers: "Wow, so what does software engineering entail? Where did you go to school for that?"

Ideally, they would ask you a question in return. But if they don't and you run out of topical conversation about their life, try these:

- "I've been reading a lot of fiction lately. Do you have a favorite fiction book? Why do you love it?"
- "What's a book/movie you hate that everyone else likes?" (or vice versa)
- "What surprised you most about your current job?"
- "What was your first job? Did you like it?"
- "Do you have a favorite spot in this area? One we don't know about?"
- "I've been wanting to try a new restaurant here. Do you have a favorite?"
- Couples: "How did you guys meet? What drew you to him/her? Tell us your love story."
- "I've been thinking about _____. Have you read/thought about that? What are your thoughts?"
- "What's the best piece of advice you've ever received?" (You can ask this in context of work, marriage, parenting, and so on).

Going "deep" is normal in the Masonheimer home . . . maybe a little too much! We often talk about religion, current events, church, parenting, Scripture, and culture as naturally as breathing.

Because this is normalized in our home, our conversations naturally bend that direction. But all deep talk starts with small talk, and you have to lay a foundation of inconsequential questions for people to feel safe opening up. Don't knock small talk—get good at it, and the deep stuff will come with time.

It won't be perfect, and that's the point. We don't preach the gospel through perfect lives. We preach the gospel through real ones. This doesn't require you to let your house fall apart or fail to tend to the needs of your home; it requires balance, discipline, and a generous heart. The beautiful thing? These are achievable when we walk by the Spirit. He tells us when we need more discipline, when we need more grace, and when we need to walk right in between.

Don't wait for the perfect time or place or people. God has you and your home here for a reason. He knows what you need, and He will supply it abundantly.

A LITURGY FOR HOSPITALITY

O good and generous God:
  we worship You for Your open arms,
  Your open hands, opened on the cross
  and still open to us today.
  Your generosity is our saving hope.
  Remind us, God, that what we have is abundantly enough;
  enough to share with those in need,
  filled to overflowing, available evermore.
  There is always more with You.
  Remove our fear of scarcity and open the hands we close
  around Your gifts; remind us
  there is always more with You.
  Turn our eyes from self to others and open the door we close
  to those we do not know; teach us
  there is always more with You.
  You supply all our needs, Christ Jesus.
  Thank you.
Amen.

If You Can Find the Beauty Here

I DON'T KNOW IF THIS BOOK IS WHAT YOU EXPECTED. Probably not. John Calvin and James Arminius would shudder, perhaps, to see the word *theology* associated with cleaning routines and hospitality tips. Perhaps you found it all a bit trivial, not as theological as you hoped.

Of course, I hope not; I hope you liked it. But either way, here's what I leave you with: your daily tasks are eternally important. One day you'll wash dishes for the last time. One day you'll fold laundry and you'll never do it again. One day you'll sweep a floor and then someone else will have to do it for you, or because you no longer have need of one.

Our time on this rotating orb is limited, and usually people point this out when they want us to skip the cleaning and cooking and "boring" things. Because our time is limited, though, I think we should pay more attention to the theology of our daily tasks. We only have one life, and they're part of it. Don't they deserve our best? Perhaps in the bending to do what is boring we learn what is eternal: patience, love, faithfulness, restraint.

There are many more glamorous ways to learn these things, but

Epilogue

I've found I learn them best in the unseen places, when they're done so people can join me at a table and find beauty where they thought none existed before. I want to be part of what God is doing in and through my home, and I believe the world will be transformed, not by more people on stages but by more people on mission, starting on the kitchen floor.

> If you can find beauty here
> you can find it anywhere.
> The trees are bare, they reach, many fingered,
> to a bluebonnet sky. And snow comes
> but never stays: settling in the cuts
> the plow made . . .
> A kind of healing in the running scars.
> What grew there once is stacked in rows,
> chopped up in piles so we last the winter.
> Not lost or gone; transformed
> from beauty to substance
> in its own way, beautiful too.
> The cold echoes in my ears,
> the layered hills from brown to purple turn
> in the leaving light, but I—
> I walk to another gleam: warm and yellow,
> a candle in a window, the lamp by the stove,
> the dark and cold a backdrop to home.
> You can find it anywhere, the beauty here;
> settling in the cuts your life made.
> "THE CUTS YOUR LIFE MADE," *PDM*

Bonus Material

HOSTING WITH YOUNG CHILDREN

When Jesus ascended, His last command was to make disciples of all nations (Matthew 28:19–20). When you're a parent of young kids, leaving to disciple people in a foreign country probably isn't on your agenda; your primary discipleship is to the little people under your roof. But you also have another mission field—the one outside your door:

- your neighborhood
- your street
- your town
- your church

These people are in our lives for a reason. As followers of Jesus, we are called to share Christ with them through our words and our lives. And, as we've discussed so far, one of the best ways to do this is by opening our homes.

As a teen I watched my parents (both introverts) open their door over and over, host and invite and live out hospitality even when it wasn't reciprocated. I remember my mom stacking piles of dishes by the sink, saying: "You may do 80 percent of the inviting and only 20 percent of the time get invited to your guests' homes. Invite anyway." My parents didn't have an example of hospitality in their families of origin. They started something new based on Scripture's call to outward-facing love.

Josh and I dedicated ourselves to sharing the home God gave us, whatever its size. Early in our marriage, at the height of toddler parenting, people were in our home two to five times a week for parties, dinners, or simply stopping by (we lived in town). Though we're no longer hosting that often (and I'm not sure I recommend it), we learned a lot about hospitality while parenting very small kids. In our current season—running a business together, co-homeschooling, managing a farm—we host less often, but it's on the calendar every week. At the time I'm writing this book our kids are eight, six, and three—still quite small. But they are as much a part of the hospitality as we are.

Small kids have high energy, and when you get to bedtime, hosting might be the last thing you want to do. But community ultimately brings us life and brings life to others. God knows this. The reward of hospitality manifests long term. Here is how to open your home while parenting littles—from people who've spent our entire hospitality experience with small children. Having your children there to observe hospitality as your *norm* will transform their own view of this biblical pursuit—just as it did for me.

CHANGE YOUR MINDSET

To open your home when your kids are small you must let go of perfectionism. If you are only willing to open your home when it looks like a Pinterest picture, you'll never do it. Jesus isn't calling us to put together perfect homes. He's calling us to emulate Him, opening our arms and our tables to the people He has purposely put into our lives.

This shift requires a thought exchange:

- Exchanging pursuit of perfection for pursuit of generosity. A perfectionist is more concerned with everything being *right* instead of everyone being *blessed*. A generous person realizes people don't care what everything looks and tastes like if the community meets their deepest needs.

- Exchanging fear of man for reverence for God. If you fear the opinions of people, you'll spend the whole night worried about what they think of your house, food, and you. But if you serve others out of love for God, you'll be released from that pressure.

- Exchanging a desire to control for a desire to love others. A controlling spirit tries to make everything go according to plan, usually to maintain appearances (attempting to control others' opinions). When you open your home with only one motive—to love others—you're released from the need to control. This is the most freeing of the three mental exchanges because it will also change how you treat your kids. You're less likely to "lose it" when getting ready to host because they're no longer variables who mess up a controlled environment.

ESTABLISH FREEING ROUTINES

Remember: discipline brings freedom. The more solid your routines, the easier hosting will be. Those cleaning routines you put in place? They save you when you open the door. You don't have to "catch up" because the little you do every day helps you stay on top of things. When it comes time to host, there is no whole-house-cleaning-spree because the house never falls that far behind. Pick up a few toys, start the food (or order pizza), and do a quick skim of the living room and bathroom. Close the door on the playroom and just ignore it—who's going in there?! Focus on the areas for guests only.

PS: There is no such thing as a superhost. Every superhost has simply learned to manage time and home in a way that makes life easier. Establish routines that work for you, and you'll be surprised how easy it is.

OPEN OFTEN AND IMPERFECTLY

If you wait for the perfect time, house, kids, or community, you will never open your home. And if you never open your home, you'll never engage with the very people who need to see Christ in you.

The biggest reason my introverted husband is willing to open our home so regularly is because he sees the mission behind it. Hospitality is ministry. Whether it's hosting overnight guests in our playroom turned guest room, or hosting a weekly Bible study, or inviting couples to dinner, or setting up an at-home play date with the girls' cousins, opening our home often breaks the need for everything to be perfect. You can't maintain perfection when you're opening a real, lived-in home twice a week (or more). Practice makes perfect.

DO NOT FEAR BOUNDARIES

Hospitality is wonderful, but it has boundaries. Our door is open, but not all the time. We still have work to do, kids to educate, and a home to run. The constant interruptions of our house in town got so bad, I put a sign on the door that I was in "Office Hours." My mother—who home educated—put up a sign that said "School in Session" for the same reason. It is okay to have boundaries on when people can come to your home. It is your home, not theirs. People can respect your family (or personal) schedule.

For example, when people ask if they can stop by, I usually ask them to come at lunch. This way I can complete our homeschool routine, but I can still get to work during my office hours. This is not selfish; my children need school, and I need to work. But I can also make time to see a soul God loves by offering a few different times. If you are working from home (or even a stay-at-home mom who needs afternoons for home tasks), you have the right to protect certain time frames for the good of your family and calendar. There will be days this can't happen, but those days should not be the norm.

Good hospitality happens within structure and boundaries. Otherwise, it can't be emotionally maintained.

RAISE HOSPITABLE KIDS

Involve your children in the hosting process. Have them stay in the room when you converse with the adults, greet each person who comes in, and sit at the table for dinner. My girls have been in rooms of twenty-plus rowdy adults during our Bible study nights. They've been passed around a campfire as we roasted marshmallows into the late summer nights in Michigan with friends. They sit at the table when friends stop by for coffee. They are part of our missional family journey.

It's so important for children in Christian homes to understand that our faith is not just *inward* but *outward*. Children must see that faith is meant to spur evangelism, and evangelism begins in the home.

One of the best illustrations of this was when we lived in the little house in town. One of my friends swung by to say hi during lunchtime and one of my children—in the throes of potty training—proudly handed her a bowl of her own pee. Nothing says, "Welcome to our real life!" like a potty full of urine.

LIVE OUT THE GOSPEL

There is a famous saying: "Preach Christ, and if you must, use words." Our lives should preach the gospel. And when they do, our kids see it. When you have small kids, a wonderful way to live and speak the gospel to the people God has entrusted to your life is to open up your home.

A few ways we do this:

- Learn our neighbors' names and bring gifts at major holidays.
- Host weekly Bible studies in our home.
- Invite couples and families to dinner once a week (we set aside a day).
- Host pizza parties for the college students at our church.
- Set up outings with other couples when we can get a babysitter.
- Coordinate coffee dates one-on-one.
- Host mini parties for groups of friends and invite newer community members over to meet them.
- Host an annual Hobbit Party, where we dress up in Lord of the Rings attire, set up a tent, haybales, and charcuterie boards with snacks.
- Host an annual homeschool harvest party for our co-op, with a hayride, apple bobbing, donut-eating contest, and sack races.
- Host an end of year "New Year's Eve of Eve" party, where we sing hymns and "Auld Lang Syne" together and do a kids' gingerbread house competition.

BOOKS TO INCITE A LOVE
AND VISION FOR HOME

If you struggle to visualize what a beautiful, loving home could look like, a picture is worth a thousand words. Since you've already read many thousands of words in this book, pictures are a natural next step! Following are some books that shaped my own view of home and what it could be. Some of these are children's books, but the artistic renderings and stories are so lovely I recommend them even to adults. Each book includes beautiful stories of quality relationships, vibrant colors, delicious foods, lovely nature scenes, and laughter to inspire your vision for what home can be. At the bottom I've included some adult reading if you want to dive deeper into this topic.

Children's Books:

- *Apple Picking Time* by Michele Benoit Slawson
- *The Doorbell Rang* by Pat Hutchins
- *Cranberry Thanksgiving* by Wende and Harry Devlin
- *Blueberries for Sal* by Robert McCloskey
- *Hailstones and Halibut Bones* by Mary O'Neill
- *Roxaboxen* by Alice McLerran
- *Miss Rumphius* by Barbara Cooney
- *Barn Dance!* by Bill Martin Jr. and John Archambault
- *The Keeping Quilt* by Patricia Polacco
- *Thunder Cake* by Patricia Polacco
- *Winter Days in the Big Woods* by Laura Ingalls Wilder
- *The Rainbabies* by Laura Krauss Melmed
- *In November* by Cynthia Rylant
- *The Seven Silly Eaters* by Mary Ann Hoberman
- *All the Places to Love* by Patricia MacLachlan (my favorite!)
- *Sleep Tight Farm* by Eugenie Doyle
- *Night Is Coming* by W. Nikola-Lisa
- *Letting Swift River Go* by Jane Yolen
- *The True Princess* by Angela Elwell Hunt

Books for Adults:

- *Holy Hygge: Creating a Place for People to Gather and the Gospel to Grow* by Jamie Erickson
- *The Hidden Art of Homemaking: Creative Ideas for Enriching Everyday Life* by Edith Schaeffer
- *Reach Out, Gather In: 40 Days to Opening Your Heart and Home* by Karen Ehman

Bonus Material

- *The Gospel Comes with a House Key: Practicing Radically Ordinary Hospitality in Our Post-Christian World* by Rosaria Butterfield
- *Home Comforts: The Art and Science of Keeping House* by Cheryl Mendelson

Acknowledgments

I WANT TO EXTEND A HEARTFELT THANK-YOU TO EVERY-
one who worked on this project: to Stephanie, Brooke, Lisa-Jo,
and Kathleen, without whose input and wisdom the book would
not have come together. I feel immensely grateful to write a book
about home in a more unique way—including poetry, liturgies, *and*
cleaning routines—with editors and agents who truly believed in
the project.

I also want to thank my parents for building a home (physically
and spiritually) worth emulating. My "frentors" (friend-mentors)
Karen and Lisa have built on that foundation with their unique
wisdom and experience at home, helping me grow as a Christian,
wife, mother, and minister. My colleagues and peers in ministry
have also played an important role in my vision for home beyond
the borders of my city, state, stage of life, and ethnicity—a gift I
appreciate daily.

My local community has been a rock and an example of how to
love well, connect deeply, and build a strong homelife in all seasons.
They have given me grace (especially during the edits of this book!)
and have given me support, and most of all have given me a vision
for what is possible in community when people base their lives on
the affection of God.

Acknowledgments

Last but certainly not least, I am thankful for my husband, Josh, and my three sweet children, without whom this home would be empty. They bring it to life with their laughter and messes, their joys and sorrows. I hope, years from now, they look back on our home as a place where the things I've written were always lived out loud.

Notes

CHAPTER 1

1. Adriana Reyes, Robert F. Schoeni, and HwaJung Choi, "Race/Ethnic Differences in Spatial Distance Between Adult Children and Their Mothers," *Journal of Marriage and Family* 82, no. 2 (April 2020): 810–21, Wiley Online Library, https://doi.org/10.1111/jomf.12614.

2. Chloe Gray, "Why These Household Skills Might Be Dying Out," *Good Housekeeping*, January 30, 2018, https://www.goodhousekeeping .com/uk/house-and-home/household-advice/a575102/the-household -skills-were-losing/.

3. John Tweeddale, "A Theology of the Home," Ligonier, June 22, 2020, https://www.ligonier.org/learn/articles/theology-home.

CHAPTER 2

1. Henry Blackaby, Richard Blackaby, and Claude King, *Experiencing God: Knowing and Doing the Will of God* (Nashville: B&H Publishing Group, 2008), 147.

CHAPTER 3

1. *Merriam-Webster*, s.v. "discipline," accessed May 24, 2024, https://www .merriam-webster.com/dictionary/discipline#did-you-know.

CHAPTER 4

1. Claire M. Kamp Dush, Kammi K. Schmeer, and Miles Taylor, "Chaos as a Social Determinant of Child Health: Reciprocal Associations?" *Social Science & Medicine* 95 (October 2013): 69–76, ScienceDirect, https://doi.org/10.1016/j.socscimed.2013.01.038.

2. John Bunyan, *The Pilgrim's Progress: From This World to That Which Is to Come* (Philadelphia: S. I. Bell, 1891).

Notes

CHAPTER 5

1. Leah Boden, *Modern Miss Mason: Discover How Charlotte Mason's Revolutionary Ideas on Home Education Can Change How You and Your Children Learn and Grow Together* (Carol Stream, IL: Tyndale Momentum, 2023), 33.
2. Oxford Languages, *Oxford English Dictionary*, s.v. "culture," accessed May 24, 2024, Google search.
3. Rod Dreher, *The Benedict Option: A Strategy for Christians in a Post-Christian Nation* (New York: Sentinel, 2017), 108.
4. Dreher, *The Benedict Option*, 108.

CHAPTER 6

1. "Matthew Henry Commentary on the Whole Bible (Complete): 1 Corinthians 10," Bible Study Tools, Salem Media Group, accessed November 14, 2023, https://www.biblestudytools.com/commentaries /matthew-henry-complete/1-corinthians/10.html.
2. David Guzik, "1 Corinthians 10—Idolatry Then and Now," Enduring Word, 2018, https://enduringword.com/bible-commentary/1-corinthians-10/.
3. Sara Hagerty, *Unseen: The Gift of Being Hidden in a World That Loves to Be Noticed* (Grand Rapids, MI: Zondervan, 2017), 29.

CHAPTER 7

1. L. M. Montgomery, *Anne of Avonlea* (1909, repr., London: Macmillan Collector's Library, 2020), 177.
2. Tish Harrison Warren, *Liturgy of the Ordinary: Sacred Practices in Everyday Life* (Downers Grove, IL: IVP Books, 2016), 34.
3. Rod Dreher, *The Benedict Option: A Strategy for Christians in a Post-Christian Nation* (New York: Sentinel, 2017), 108.
4. Sally Clarkson and Sarah Clarkson, *The Lifegiving Home: Creating a Place of Belonging and Becoming* (Carol Stream, IL: Tyndale Momentum, 2016), 10–11.
5. Richard Foster, *Celebration of Discipline: The Path to Spiritual Growth* (San Francisco: Harper & Row, 1978).
6. Glenna Marshall, *Memorizing Scripture: The Basics, Blessings, and Benefits of Meditating on God's Word* (Chicago: Moody Publishers, 2023), 27.
7. "The Pomodoro Technique," The Pomodoro Technique, Combinant Dynamics Consulting, accessed May 25, 2024, https://www .pomodorotechnique.com/.
8. Charlotte Mason, *Home Education: The Original Homeschooling Guide* (1886, repr., Brattleboro, VT: Echo Point Books & Media, 2022), 107.

CHAPTER 10

1. Laura Ingalls Wilder, *Little House in the Big Woods* (New York: Harper & Brothers, 1932), 16.

CHAPTER 11

1. Richard Thompson, "Gardening for Health: A Regular Dose of Gardening," *Clinical Medicine* 18, no. 3 (June 2018): 201–5, ScienceDirect, https://doi.org/10.7861/clinmedicine.18-3-201.

CHAPTER 13

1. *Strong's Concordance*, s.v. "philoxenia," Blue Letter Bible, accessed May 25, 2024, https://www.blueletterbible.org/lexicon/g5381/kjv/tr/0-1/.

2. Amy Novotney, "The Risks of Social Isolation," *Monitor on Psychology* 50, no. 5 (May 2019): 32, American Psychological Association, https://www.apa.org/monitor/2019/05/ce-corner-isolation.

3. Daniel A. Cox, "Men's Social Circles are Shrinking," Survey Center on American Life, American Enterprise Institute, June 29, 2021, https://www.americansurveycenter.org/why-mens-social-circles-are-shrinking/.

4. C. S. Lewis, *The Four Loves* (New York: Harcourt Brace Jovanovich, 1960), 169.

5. Henry Cloud and John Townsend, *Making Small Groups Work: What Every Small Group Leader Needs to Know* (Grand Rapids, MI: Zondervan, 2003), 45.

About the Author

PHYLICIA MASONHEIMER IS A BESTSELLING AUTHOR, Bible teacher, and host of the *Verity* podcast. She is the founder of Every Woman a Theologian, an organization teaching Christians how to know what they believe, why they believe it, and how to live their faith authentically in the world. Phylicia loves good books, black coffee, goats, and gardening. She lives on a northern Michigan farm with her husband, Josh, and their three children: Adeline, Geneva, and Ivan.

Also available by Phylicia Masonheimer

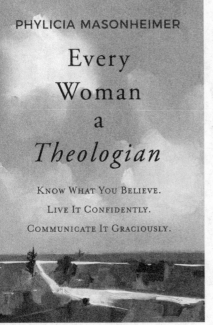

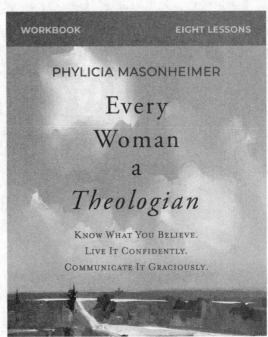